Pressing On
When the Pressure's On

A Bible Study Workbook on Perseverance for Ages 6-12

Life Changer Bible Study Series

Cheryl L. Crane

iUniverse, Inc.
New York Bloomington

Pressing On When the Pressure's On
A Bible Study Workbook on Perseverance for Ages 6-12

All Scripture quotations are taken from the HOLY BIBLE, NEW INTERNATIONAL VERSION ®, NIV ®. Copyright © 1973, 1978, 1984, 1985 by International Bible Society. Used by permission of Zondervan.

Cover art and illustrations by Josh Shelton.

iUniverse books may be ordered through booksellers or by contacting:

iUniverse
1663 Liberty Drive
Bloomington, IN 47403
www.iuniverse.com
1-800-Authors (1-800-288-4677)

Because of the dynamic nature of the Internet, any Web addresses or links contained in this book may have changed since publication and may no longer be valid. The views expressed in this work are solely those of the author and do not necessarily reflect the views of the publisher, and the publisher hereby disclaims any responsibility for them.

ISBN: 978-1-4401-5830-8 (pbk)
ISBN: 978-1-4401-5831-5 (ebk)

Printed in the United States of America

iUniverse rev. date: 7/23/2009

Dedicated to...

the believing hearts,
the praying hands,
the encouraging voices
of faithful family and friends.

**Let us not become weary in doing good,
for at the proper time we will reap a harvest
if we do not give up.**

Galations 6:9

Contents

Note to Parents & Teachers

Somewhere I read, "How can any of us be at ease when there are billions of people who have not yet heard the gospel?" My heart cries, "How can any of us be at ease when there are so many people living in the lie that God's Word is boring and irrelevant to their lives?" Life Changers Bible studies shatter that lie with the truth of God's Word.

Daily Questions lead students to discover who God is and how He expects us to live. Mind Changers sections help students think about what God is saying to them personally. Students decide how their thoughts or actions should change to better follow Him.

Group Discussion is the final step in helping students become doers of the Word, not just hearers. As parent or teacher, you choose the format. Students can discuss an entire lesson at a time after completing a whole week's work or reinforce lessons learned daily by sharing answers right after finishing each day's pages. If you know the Bible well, you may be comfortable just inviting students to share their answers in the group. If you'd rather have the answers, read on.

A Free Answer Key is available at **www.Life-ChangingWords.com.** Just click on **Books\Resources.** Scroll down to this book's summary. Click **download** and follow the prompts to download the free pdf file. Along with answers, it includes additional questions you can use to spark deeper discussions or as journaling ideas for older students.

This study is generally for ages 6 to 12; please adapt it for your children. Read to younger ones if need be. Older students can lead discussions! Watch God grow spiritual leaders.

This study does not assume that every student has a personal relationship with Jesus Christ. Throughout the lessons, there are invitations for students to read pages 93 and 94, pray and accept Jesus as Savior. They are then encouraged to tell a parent. May there be much rejoicing in families as students share decisions to follow Christ and are discipled to grow in the Lord.

Hey Kids: Why Change Your Mind Anyway?

God's Orders

Yup. Jesus commands us to. He said, "Do not conform any longer to the pattern of this world, but be transformed by the renewing of your mind." (Romans 12:2) "Transformed" means changed. Jesus wants us to change our minds to line up more with His. Now I'm guessing that if you have this book in your hands – and Mom didn't make you read it – you're at least curious about Jesus. Maybe you've already accepted Him as your Savior. (If not, there's more about that on pages 93 and 94.)

Asking Jesus to be our Savior, to forgive us for wrong things – or sins – that we've done, is only Step 1. What's Step 2? From the moment we pray and ask Him to lead our lives, we should start becoming like Him. **No one truly follows Jesus without changing.**

Sin is U-G-L-Y

You see, when we ask Jesus for forgiveness, we are sinners seeking after a perfect God. Even in human form, God never did anything wrong. Jesus never talked back to His Dad or hit His brother. He is perfect. To Him our sin is repulsive. What's repulsive? Imagine the bottom of a smelly tin garbage can on a hot summer day. Picture rotten brown bananas mixed with chunky sour milk and a few worms in the muck eating it all. Yuck! That's how we look to God *before* we accept Jesus. God is holy; our sin is garbage.

After we decide to accept Jesus as our Savior, we must change and sin less. If we cooperate with the Holy Spirit, we'll become more like Jesus. More loving. More forgiving. **And better able to persevere in doing what He wants.**

Your Head Drives Your Heart

Change begins in our thinking. Jesus tells all who accept Him, "be made new in the attitude of your minds." Only God's Word can renew our minds. Everyday we need to talk and listen to Jesus (pray), read His Word (the Bible) and let the Holy Spirit change our thoughts to be more like His. As our minds focus on God, better actions will follow.

We "let" the Holy Spirit change us in our daily choices. Choosing God's ways over ours makes us more like Him. For example, the Bible says that we should do everything as if working for the Lord and not for people. Think about a new school year. At the start you want to do your best, working carefully on your math problems and writing full sentences neatly on your papers. But later you may get tired and want to take shortcuts. Do not grow weary in doing good, for at the proper time you will reap a harvest if you do not give up. (Galations 6:9) You have a choice. Will you get sloppy or press on and keep doing your best like Jesus wants? Persevering to do your best makes you more like Jesus.

Focus: Perseverance

Perseverance is stick-to-it-iveness. It drives marathon runners to press on for 26 pounding miles. It empowers brave soldiers to defend their country against danger day after day. It enables the school spelling bee champ to practice those word lists week after week after week, right up to the morning of the competition.

Where does perseverance come from and what does it look like in your life? Find out as you join the adventures of warrior Joshua, prophet Elijah and others who took hold of the work God had for them and stuck to it like flies on syrup-covered pancakes. Then you, too, will be ready to press on when the pressure's on!

☺ Remember to pray before you begin. Ask the Holy Spirit to teach you what He has for you each time you study His Word. Did you know that guiding us into truth is His job? Read John 16:13 to see. After studying, ask God to help you live what you learn.

✎ Look for places to write down what God is teaching you, where you need to change and the steps you'll take to think and act more like Jesus. God is waiting to reveal some special lessons just for you.

Let's get started!

 Meet Wordsly Hi! I'm Wordsly, a friendly bookworm who loves God's Word and helping kids like you study it. You'll see me pop up in your pages with word definitions, Bible facts and other handy info.
My Bible or Yours? You'll find Bible verses for the whole week printed at the beginning of each lesson. And all verses used in this book are from the New International Version (NIV) Bible.

Bible Verses for Lesson 1

Joshua 7:6-13, 8:1-19

(God told Joshua to lead Israel to take over the land God promised them. Joshua obeyed and Israel won the first battle! But when they fought again at Ai, Joshua didn't know that an Israelite had sinned by stealing things belonging to God. The Ai army killed, chased and scared Israel! What a failure! What will Joshua do?)

[6] Then Joshua tore his clothes and fell facedown to the ground before the ark of the LORD, remaining there till evening. The elders of Israel did the same, and sprinkled dust on their heads. [7] And Joshua said, "Ah, Sovereign LORD, why did you ever bring this people across the Jordan to deliver us into the hands of the Amorites to destroy us? If only we had been content to stay on the other side of the Jordan! [8] O LORD, what can I say, now that Israel has been routed by its enemies? [9] The Canaanites and the other people of the country will hear about this and they will surround us and wipe out our name from the earth. What then will you do for your own great name?"

[10] The LORD said to Joshua, "Stand up! What are you doing down on your face?
[11] Israel has sinned; they have violated my covenant, which I commanded them to keep. They have taken some of the devoted things; they have stolen, they have lied, they have put them with their own possessions. [12] That is why the Israelites cannot stand against their enemies; they turn their backs and run because they have been made liable to destruction. I will not be with you anymore unless you destroy whatever among you is devoted to destruction.

[13] "Go, consecrate the people. Tell them, 'Consecrate yourselves in preparation for tomorrow; for this is what the LORD, the God of Israel, says: That which is devoted is among you, O Israel. You cannot stand against your enemies until you remove it.'"

(Joshua obeyed God, found the man who sinned and removed him from camp.)

8 [1] Then the LORD said to Joshua, "Do not be afraid; do not be discouraged. Take the whole army with you, and go up and attack Ai. For I have delivered into your hands the king of Ai, his people, his city and his land. ² You shall do to Ai and its king as you did to Jericho and its king, except that you may carry off their plunder and livestock for yourselves. Set an ambush behind the city."

³ So Joshua and the whole army moved out to attack Ai. He chose thirty thousand of his best fighting men and sent them out at night ⁴ with these orders: "Listen carefully. You are to set an ambush behind the city. Don't go very far from it. All of you be on the alert. ⁵ I and all those with me will advance on the city, and when the men come out against us, as they did before, we will flee from them. ⁶ They will pursue us until we have lured them away from the city, for they will say, 'They are running away from us as they did before.' So when we flee from them, ⁷ you are to rise up from ambush and take the city. The LORD your God will give it into your hand. ⁸ When you have taken the city, set it on fire. Do what the LORD has commanded. See to it; you have my orders."

⁹ Then Joshua sent them off, and they went to the place of ambush and lay in wait between Bethel and Ai, to the west of Ai—but Joshua spent that night with the people.

¹⁰ Early the next morning Joshua mustered his men, and he and the leaders of Israel marched before them to Ai. ¹¹ The entire force that was with him marched up and approached the city and arrived in front of it. They set up camp north of Ai, with the valley between them and the city. ¹² Joshua had taken about five thousand men and set them in ambush between Bethel and Ai, to the west of the city. ¹³ They had the soldiers take up their positions—all those in the camp to the north of the city and the ambush to the west of it. That night Joshua went into the valley.

¹⁴ When the king of Ai saw this, he and all the men of the city hurried out early in the morning to meet Israel in battle at a certain place overlooking the Arabah. But he did not know that an ambush had been set against him behind the city. ¹⁵ Joshua and all Israel let themselves be driven back before them, and they fled toward the desert. ¹⁶ All the men of Ai were called to pursue them, and they pursued Joshua and were lured away from the city. ¹⁷ Not a man remained in Ai or Bethel who did not go after Israel. They left the city open and went in pursuit of Israel.

¹⁸ Then the LORD said to Joshua, "Hold out toward Ai the javelin that is in your hand, for into your hand I will deliver the city." So Joshua held out his javelin toward Ai. ¹⁹ As soon as he did this, the men in the ambush rose quickly from their position and rushed forward. They entered the city and captured it and quickly set it on fire.

Lesson 1

Battling an Enemy:
Joshua Wins at Ai

Joshua 7:6-9
Clues like this (17) tell you the verse number where you'll find the answer.

1. Circle what Joshua did (6) after losing the first battle at Ai.

fell facedown and prayed   panicked   pouted

2. Before whom or what did Joshua fall facedown? Circle one.

the King of Ai   the Israelites   the ark of the Lord

3. Circle how long Joshua prayed.   5 minutes   till evening   a week

4. When Israel's elders saw what Joshua did, which did they do?

ran away to find a new leader   did the same as Joshua and prayed

5. Unscramble the words from the end of verse 9 that show whose reputation Joshua was most worried about. Then circle who the words refer to at the right.

1. _ _ _ _   2. _ _ _   3. _ _ _ _ _   4. _ _ _ _   God   Joshua

  R O Y U   N W O   R E T A G   E N A M

Mind Changers

1. Don't worry about Ai. Ai is gone! Circle failures below that could happen to you.

get a low grade on a school test   lose a championship game in a sport

lose a writing contest   lose a friend because you told a lie

not making a sports team   not getting a part you want in a play

miss passing to the next level in karate, skating or another class

2. If you follow Joshua's example, circle what you'll do after you have a failure.

pray   panic   pout

3. Who can you go to for help deciding what to do next? Circle all that are true.

God   parent   a pet   teacher   coach   wise friend

4. Joshua (the leader of God's people) didn't want Israel's loss to make people think God was weak. Mark an X by what you care about most.

___ what your actions make people think of <u>you</u>
___ what your actions make people think of <u>God</u>

5. Mark the one you think God wants you to care about most.

___ what your actions make people think of <u>you</u>
___ what your actions make people think of <u>God</u>

Hide His Word and Seek Him! "I have hidden your word in my heart that I might not sin against you." (Psalm 119:11) If we memorize His Word, it will help us sin less and be more like Jesus. So each lesson has a memory verse. Hide this one in your heart to get started!

Lesson 1 Memory Verse
Joshua 8:18

Then the Lord said to Joshua, "Hold out toward Ai the javelin that is in your hand, for into your hand I will deliver the city."
So Joshua held out his javelin toward Ai.

Battling an Enemy:
Joshua Wins at Ai

Joshua 7:10-13

1. Circle what happened (10-11) after Joshua prayed?

nothing   God told Joshua why Israel failed

2. Fill in the blanks (11-12) telling why Israel couldn't win against Ai.

"Israel has _____; they have violated my covenant, which I commanded
them to keep. They have taken some of the devoted things; they have _____,
they have _____, they have put them with their own possessions."

3. What did God tell Israel in the last line of verse 12?

"I will not _____ _____ _____ anymore unless you destroy whatever among
you is devoted to destruction."

Would God Leave? In verse 12, God tells Israel that He won't
be with them anymore unless they get rid of the person who sinned – the
person who was "devoted to destruction." God had to show his people
how much He hated sin. You need to know that this story happened **before**
the most amazing event in history – an event that changed the lives of people
who follow God – forever. About 2,000 years ago Jesus died on the cross to
pay for everyone's sin. He promised to be the Savior of everybody who asks
His forgiveness for their sins and chooses to follow Him. (To find out more
on that, read pages 93 & 94.) After the cross, Jesus promised His followers
that He'd never leave them nor forsake them!

4. God's Word tells us that, once we choose to follow Jesus as Savior, nothing can separate us from Him. Find the underlined words hidden in this word search.

For I am convinced that neither <u>death</u> nor <u>life</u>,
neither <u>angels</u> nor <u>demons</u>, neither the <u>present</u> nor the <u>future</u>,
nor any <u>powers</u>, neither <u>height</u> nor <u>depth</u>,
nor anything else in all creation,
will be able to separate us from the love of God
that is in Christ Jesus our Lord.   (Romans 8:38-39)

```
C  C  O  S  R  E  N  P  L  I  F  E  T  L  Y
F  D  K  C  E  T  N  O  I  M  M  E  O  Y  K
L  M  C  G  S  K  C  I  W  S  N  O  M  E  D
F  F  I  D  E  A  T  H  R  P  H  U  T  E  O
H  U  U  I  M  M  X  D  I  X  V  I  F  D  E
P  T  H  G  I  E  H  S  S  M  M  I  L  W  J
R  U  N  P  L  T  P  T  D  I  S  A  S  K  W
D  R  T  R  N  E  O  O  N  R  S  W  H  Y  P
F  E  I  L  D  S  W  P  R  E  S  E  N  T  A
W  L  U  Q  L  M  E  V  I  E  T  E  F  L  V
D  C  O  E  W  G  R  L  L  R  R  D  I  R  B
F  M  G  E  S  K  S  J  F  H  L  S  Z  A  X
P  N  C  O  T  E  W  B  W  M  D  U  L  U  Q
A  T  N  D  E  P  T  H  F  I  H  U  A  V  M
```

Mind Changers

1. Willful sin prevents a win. If we don't ask God's forgiveness for the new sins we do each day and try to stop doing them, we can have bad consequences. Circle consequences that might happen to you in the situations below.

(A) If you lie about going to a friend's house and really go to the mall…

You'll feel guilty.   Worried about getting caught, you won't enjoy shopping.

You'll lose parents' trust.   You may be grounded.

(B) If you cheat in the championship game…

You may be disqualified.   Your team may have to forfeit the game and championship.

Friends may be mad at you.   You may be banned from playing the sport.

2. Do you think Jesus is with <u>you</u> and will never leave <u>you</u>? Why or why not? (Pages 93 & 94 may help you decide.)

_____

_____

 Put the memory verse phrases in correct order. Write 1 by the first, 2 by the second, etc.

___ So Joshua held out his javelin toward Ai. Joshua 8:18

___ "Hold out toward Ai the javelin that is in your hand,

___ for into your hand I will deliver the city."

___ Then the Lord said to Joshua,

Battling an Enemy:
Joshua Wins at Ai

Joshua 8:1-12

1. After Joshua prayed and obeyed by getting rid of the sinful man who lied and stole things, what did God tell Joshua (1)?

"Do not be _____; do not be _____. Take the whole army with you and go up and attack Ai. For I have delivered into your hands the _____ of Ai, his people, his city and his land."

2. Can you find verses saying Joshua feared that Ai would beat Israel again?

     YES   NO

3. Circle the last thing God told Joshua in verse 2.

March around their wall.   Set an ambush behind the city.   Get help.

4. Find words (12) that show Joshua obeyed God's plan.

Joshua had taken about 5,000 men and _____ _____ _____ _____ between Bethel and Ai, to the west of the city.

Mind Changers

1. People who persevere in God's plan don't need to fear because God will be with them. Circle the person in each pair below who does God's will and does not need to fear.

a boy steals shoes from a store	a boy sees someone steal and tells a clerk
a girl asks a new girl if she wants to play	a girl makes fun of a new girl in school
a boy hides a student's pen as a joke	a boy lends a student a pen for a test
a girl breaks another girl's necklace	a girl replaces a necklace she broke

2. Write of a time when you felt afraid because you did something wrong and hid it.

_____

3. What can you do differently next time to do the right thing and not have to fear?

_____

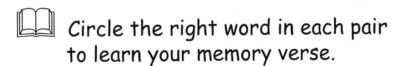 Circle the right word in each pair
to learn your memory verse.

Then the (King , Lord) said to Joshua, "Hold out toward (Ai , Bethlehem)
the (phone , javelin) that is in your (hand , ear), for into your
(mailbox , hand) I will deliver the (city , prize)."
So Joshua held out his (apple , javelin) toward Ai. (Joshua , Genesis) 8:18

Lesson 1

Day 4

Battling an Enemy:
Joshua Wins at Ai

Joshua 8:13-18

1. Persevering in God's plan meant that Joshua and his men did something unusual in their battle. Fill in the blanks to finish verse 15?

Joshua and all Israel _____ _____ _____ _____ _____
before them, and they fled toward the desert.

2. Joshua persevered. How well did the battle go? Circle T (true) or F (false).

T F Ai pursued Israel and was lured away from the city.
T F Many Israelites were killed.
T F Joshua held out his javelin when God told him to.
T F Joshua's men rushed into the city and captured it.

3. In verse 1, God promised Joshua that He would deliver Ai's king into the hands of Israel's army. By persevering, did Joshua see God's promise come true?   YES   NO

Mind Changers

1. Sometimes persevering in God's plan means stepping back before moving forward. In the situations below, circle the best "stepping back" answer.

(A)   A friend comes over yelling at you to give back a new hat that you didn't take. Which should you do?

Start yelling back immediately.   Wait till the yelling stops and then calmly say that
                                       you don't have the hat.

(B)   Friends at a party start shoving and grabbing for a candy bag. What will you do?

Wait patiently until things calm   Get in there and fight for your candy!
down and yours is handed to you.

2. As Joshua set the ambush for Ai and fought the battle, what do you think he thought about? (Circle one.)

losing the first battle to Ai   following every detail of God's plan

3. Circle everything you think God wants you to think about when you face a problem.

God's directions   past failures   the tools God has given you for success

A Puzzle to Help You Persevere

Fill in the letters to match numbers in the key below.

___   ___ ___ ___   ___ ___   ___ ___ ___ ___ ___ ___ ___ ___ ___ ___
2   7   4   17   8   1   3   16   3   13   18   6   15   2   17   14

___ ___ ___ ___ ___ ___ ___   ___ ___ ___   ___ ___ ___
6   15   13   1   5   14   15   15   2   10   19   15   1

___ ___ ___ ___ ___   ___ ___   ___ ___ ___ ___ ___ ___ ___ ___
14   2   16   3   9   10   3   9   6   13   3   17   14   6   15 .

___ ___ ___ ___ ___ ___ ___ ___ ___ ___ ___   (4:13)
11   15   2   20   2   11   11   2   4   17   9

KEY:			
1 = O	2 = I	3 = E	4 = A
5 = U	6 = T	7 = C	8 = D
9 = S	10 = M	11=P	12=F
13=R	14=G	15=H	16 = V
17=N	18=Y	19=W	20=L

📖 Write missing words to finish your memory verse.

Then the _____ said to _____, "Hold out _____ Ai

the _____ that is in your _____ ,

for into your _____ I will _____ the city."

So Joshua held out his _____ toward Ai.   Joshua ___:___

Battling an Enemy:
Joshua Wins at Ai

What did you learn from Joshua?

Read back over your answers this week. Then put an **X** in the □ by ideas that were new to you or that made you think differently about how a person who perseveres acts.

People who persevere in doing God's work...

□ 1. don't panic or pout after failures; they pray.

□ 2. humbly go to God for help.

□ 3. put God before self.

□ 4. know that willful sin can prevent a win.

□ 5. do not fear; they know God is near.

□ 6. obey God's plans exactly.

□ 7. know God guides those who persevere.

□ 8. may have to step back before moving forward.

□ 9. see God's plans work out and God's promises come true.

Put an **X** in this □ if you can say Joshua 8:18 from memory.

Bible Verses for Lesson 2

1 Samuel 1:2-18, 20, 24-28, 2:1, 11

(Elkanah's wife, Hannah, was sad. She had no children. Though Elkanah's other wife teased Hannah, she kept following God and He blessed her!)

[2] He (Elkanah) had two wives; one was called Hannah and the other Peninnah. Peninnah had children, but Hannah had none. [3] Year after year this man went up from his town to worship and sacrifice to the LORD Almighty at Shiloh, where Hophni and Phinehas, the two sons of Eli, were priests of the LORD. [4] Whenever the day came for Elkanah to sacrifice, he would give portions of the meat to his wife Peninnah and to all her sons and daughters. [5] But to Hannah he gave a double portion because he loved her, and the LORD had closed her womb. [6] And because the LORD had closed her womb, her rival kept provoking her in order to irritate her. [7] This went on year after year. Whenever Hannah went up to the house of the LORD, her rival provoked her till she wept and would not eat. [8] Elkanah her husband would say to her, "Hannah, why are you weeping? Why don't you eat? Why are you downhearted? Don't I mean more to you than ten sons?"

[9] Once when they had finished eating and drinking in Shiloh, Hannah stood up. Now Eli the priest was sitting on a chair by the doorpost of the LORD's temple. [10] In bitterness of soul Hannah wept much and prayed to the LORD. [11] And she made a vow, saying, "O LORD Almighty, if you will only look upon your servant's misery and remember me, and not forget your servant but give her a son, then I will give him to the LORD for all the days of his life, and no razor will ever be used on his head." [12] As she kept on praying to the LORD, Eli observed her mouth. [13] Hannah was praying in her heart, and her lips were moving but her voice was not heard. Eli thought she was drunk [14] and said to her, "How long will you keep on getting drunk? Get rid of your wine."

[15] "Not so, my lord," Hannah replied, "I am a woman who is deeply troubled. I have not been drinking wine or beer; I was pouring out my soul to the LORD. [16] Do not take your servant for a wicked woman; I have been praying here out of my great anguish and grief."

[17] Eli answered, "Go in peace, and may the God of Israel grant you what you have asked of him." [18] She said, "May your servant find favor in your eyes." Then she went her way and ate something, and her face was no longer downcast.

[20] So in the course of time Hannah conceived and gave birth to a son. She named him Samuel, saying, "Because I asked the LORD for him."

²⁴ After he was weaned, she took the boy with her, young as he was, along with a three-year-old bull, an ephah of flour and a skin of wine, and brought him to the house of the LORD at Shiloh. ²⁵ When they had slaughtered the bull, they brought the boy to Eli, ²⁶ and she said to him, "As surely as you live, my lord, I am the woman who stood here beside you praying to the LORD. ²⁷ I prayed for this child, and the LORD has granted me what I asked of him. ²⁸ So now I give him to the LORD. For his whole life he will be given over to the LORD." And he worshiped the LORD there.

2   ¹ Then Hannah prayed and said:
    "My heart rejoices in the LORD;
    in the LORD my horn is lifted high.
    My mouth boasts over my enemies,
    for I delight in your deliverance."

¹¹ Then Elkanah went home to Ramah, but the boy ministered before the LORD under Eli the priest.

Lesson 2

Beating a Bully:
Hannah Prays Away a Problem
1 Samuel 1:1-5

Why 2 Wives?! Well, it wasn't God's idea! God's perfect plan since Adam and Eve was for one man to marry one woman for as long as they live, but people don't always follow God's plan. Elkanah loved Hannah, but probably married Peninnah, too, when Hannah couldn't have children. Though having two wives was and is wrong, it was a custom in that day. As you can see, not living by God's plan for marriage causes all kinds of problems!

1. What did Elkanah and Hannah have a good habit of doing; how often did they go (3)?

_____ _____ _____ this man went up from his town to _____

and sacrifice to the _____ _____ at Shiloh, where Hophni and Phinehas, the two sons of Eli were priests of the LORD.

2. Circle the things you think Hannah gained from worshipping God regularly.

tired feet   hope   stronger faith in God   patience to wait on God to act

3. Circle the blessings Hannah received during this tough time (5).

a double portion of food   her husband loved her   gift card to her favorite store

Mind Changers

1. Worshipping God can give us strength, hope and patience to face hard times. Mark how often you worship God by praying, singing or attending church.

__ daily   __ weekly   __ once in awhile   __ once a year   __ never

2. Mark how often you think God wants you to worship Him.

__ daily   __ weekly   __ once in awhile   __ once a year   __ never

3. Write blessings God gave you when you faced a hard time. Think about problems with friends, big school projects or tests, moves or other hard family times.

_____

_____

Cherished Children Not having children broke Hannah's heart and hurt her reputation. In that day, not having children was thought to be a curse – something bad that happened as a punishment from God. However, then and now, it's not true to say that married couples cannot have babies because God is mad at them. Even today, some people can't have children because of sickness or past injury. The important thing to know is that children are a precious blessing from God and ultimately God is the only One who has the power to give life.

Lesson 2 Memory Verse
1 Samuel 1:27

"I prayed for this child, and the Lord has granted me what I asked of him."

Lesson 2

Beating a Bully:
Hannah Prays Away a Problem

1 Samuel 1:6-14

Really Mean Rival Poor Hannah! First neighbors looked down on her because she had no children. Second, she had to live in the same family and share her husband with a competing wife or rival who provoked her by rubbing it in! Like Hannah, we face hard times in life, but God promises that if we follow Him they won't last forever. "And the God of all grace, who called you to His eternal glory in Christ, after you have suffered a little while, will Himself restore you and make you strong, firm and steadfast." (1 Peter 5:10)

1. "Closed her womb" is a way to say Hannah could not have children. Knowing that, circle two hard and sad things (6) through which Hannah had to persevere.

Her husband did not love her   she couldn't have children   her rival provoked her

2. Circle the words you think Hannah thought as Peninnah teased her for being childless.

I can't give my husband children so I'm a worthless failure.   I have no purpose.

I can enjoy Peninnah's children since she's so kind and nice to me.

3. Write the words (6-7) showing that Hannah put up with this problem for a long time.

And because the Lord had closed her womb, her rival _____ _____ her in

order to irritate her. This went on _____ _____ _____ . Whenever

Hannah went up to the house of the Lord, her rival _____ her till

she _____ and would not _____ .

4. Circle things Hannah did as she took her problem to God in verses 9-14.

taped Peninnah's mouth shut   stood respectfully before God   wept much

threw a temper tantrum   prayed to the Lord   hit Peninnah

prayed in her heart   made a promise to God   yelled

Mind Changers

1. Circle all the hard things through which you have had to persevere or write in others.

accused of a crime you didn't do   lost a friend   moved to a new home

had a serious sickness   lost a pet   changed schools

_____

2. Circle what's true. God's strong enough to help me persevere through a problem for:

   5 minutes   5 hours   5 days   5 months   5 years

3. If you have asked Jesus to forgive you for doing wrong things and to be your Savior (see pages 93 & 94), He loves you! You are special to Him whether you do big things in your life or not. This truth alone should give you strength! To help you think this through, write T (true) or F (false) by the ideas below.

___ If you follow Jesus, "The Lord your God has chosen you out of all the peoples on the face of the earth to be His people, His treasured possession." (Deuteronomy 7:6)

___ Jesus loves people who have important jobs more than other people.

___ for, "Everyone who calls on the name of the Lord will be saved." (Romans 10:13) Jesus loves completely everyone who follows Him.

___ Even if you follow Jesus, He won't love you if you're not rich, famous and powerful.

___ Jesus is perfect and can only love His children perfectly – no more, no less.

4. Circle everything you think God wants you to do if a bully bothers you.

tape his/her mouth shut   use words   tell an adult

go boldy to God   throw a temper tantrum   pray to the Lord

stand respectfully or kneel to God   pray big words   yell at God

tell God how you feel   beat up the person   pray for the bully

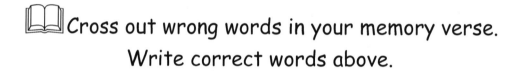Cross out wrong words in your memory verse.
Write correct words above.

"I prayed for this frog, and the Lord has knitted me what I asked of him."

1 Sandcastle 1:27

Beating a Bully:
Hannah Prays Away a Problem

1 Samuel 1:11-20

1. In the beginning of Hannah's vow, or promise (11), what did she call herself in relationship to God?

"O Lord Almighty, if you will only look upon your _____'s misery and remember me, and not forget your _____ but give her a son,"

2. Circle the best definition of the word you just wrote in question 1.

one who is in charge of everything   one who completely obeys the master

one who has power over a household   one who rides a surfboard

3. Was Hannah fully surrendered to God, no matter what happened?   YES   NO

4. If given a son, was Hannah willing to let him serve God?   YES   NO

5. Circle everything that Hannah said was true about herself (15-16). She…

was drunk.   was deeply troubled.   was sleepy.

poured out her soul to the Lord.   was wicked.   was praying.

6. Circle all blessings Hannah received because she told Eli the truth.

Eli gave her candy.   Eli said, "Go in peace."   Eli threw her a party.

Eli asked that God would grant what she asked.   Eli gave her money.

7. From the last sentence in verse 18, write words showing Hannah found peace after praying.

Then she went her way and _____ something, and her face was no longer _____.

Play the Name Game

Unscramble each name. Write the letters in the boxes on the lines with matching numbers below to discover something important that Hannah did when she named her son Samuel.

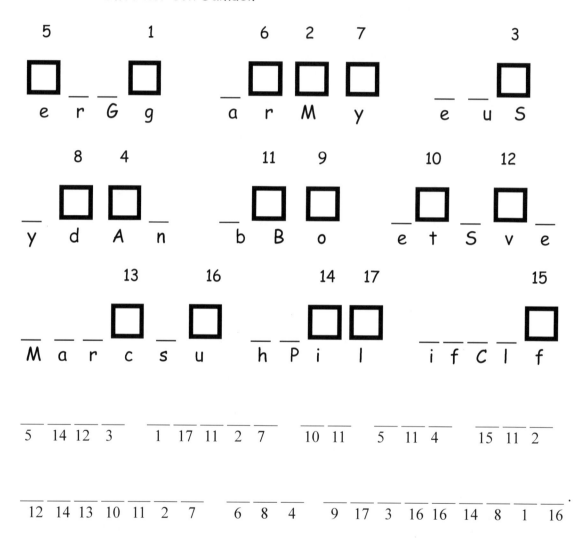

Mind Changers

1. If you are a servant of God, mark below all statements that are true.

___ I pray to God each day.   ___ I worship God at church each week.

___ I tell others about God.   ___ I read my Bible looking for God's direction.

___ I try to obey what God tells me to do.

2. Mark which things you plan to start doing this week.

___ Pray to God each day.   ___ Worship God at church each week.

___ Tell others about God.   ___ Read my Bible looking for God's direction.

___ Try to obey what God tells me to do.

3. If God gave Hannah the gift of a son, she was willing to let her son serve God. Circle everything of yours that you are willing to let God use.

your time   your mouth to speak His truth   your knees to pray on

your allowance   your eyes to read your Bible   your hands to help others

4. Write a blessing you received at a time when you told the truth. OR write one thing that you need to tell the truth about now.

_____

Circle the right word in each pair in your memory verse.

"I (sang , prayed) for this (child , puppy) and the (Lord , angel) has granted me what I asked of him."   1 Samuel 1:27

Lesson 2

Day 4

Beating a Bully:
Hannah Prays Away a Problem

1 Samuel 1:24-28, 2:1, 11

1. Write words that show Hannah gave glory to God (27).

I _____ for this child, and the Lord has _____ me what I asked of him.

2. Write words showing that Hannah wholeheartedly kept her promise to God (28).

So now I _____ him to the Lord. For his _____ life he will be _____ over to the Lord. And he worshiped the Lord there.

Do I Have to Move to the Temple? No! You don't have to move into a temple to serve God. There are lots of people who need to know about God right where you live. Samuel's case was unusual. While God can ask people to move to different places to serve Him, He often asks us to serve Him right where we are!

3. Circle all that happened because Hannah persevered in prayer. (1:26-28, 2:1, 11)

Samuel learned to worship God.

Hannah won $1,000.

Hannah rejoiced in the Lord.

Peninnah lost her voice.

Eli saw the power of God to answer prayer.

God gained another servant -- Samuel.

God was honored when Hannah kept her word that Samuel would serve the Lord.

Mind Changers

1. What prayer of yours has God answered lately? _____

2. Write one good thing God has done in your life. _____

3. Write the name of one person you can tell about this. _____

4. Circle when you plan to tell him or her.

today   tomorrow   before next week   next week

📖 Write missing words to finish your memory verse.

"I _____ for this child and the _____ has granted me what I

_____ of him."   1 _____ 1:27

Beating a Bully:
Hannah Prays Away a Problem

What did you learn from Hannah?

Read back over your answers this week. Then put an **X** in the ☐ by ideas that were new to you or that made you think differently about how a person who perseveres acts.

People who persevere in doing God's work...

☐ 1. gain strength from regularly worshiping God.

☐ 2. look for God's blessings in hard times.

☐ 3. trust God that the problem won't go on forever.

☐ 4. know God values His people for who they are, not what they do.

☐ 5. pray all the way through problems.

☐ 6. fully surrender themselves and their gifts to God.

☐ 7. find peace in prayer.

☐ 8. glorify God by telling others what He's done.

☐ 9. inspire others to worship and serve God.

Put an **X** in this ☐ if you can say 1 Samuel 1:27 from memory.

Bible Verses for Lesson 3

1 Kings 18:16-39

(Bad King Ahab and Queen Jezebel turned Israel away from God to worship false gods. The evil rulers were out to kill God's prophets -- like Elijah. So far he had escaped, but Elijah was about to meet with King Ahab.)

[16] So Obadiah went to meet Ahab and told him, and Ahab went to meet Elijah. [17] When he saw Elijah, he said to him, "Is that you, you troubler of Israel?"

[18] "I have not made trouble for Israel," Elijah replied. "But you and your father's family have. You have abandoned the LORD's commands and have followed the Baals. [19] Now summon the people from all over Israel to meet me on Mount Carmel. And bring the four hundred and fifty prophets of Baal and the four hundred prophets of Asherah, who eat at Jezebel's table." [20] So Ahab sent word throughout all Israel and assembled the prophets on Mount Carmel. [21] Elijah went before the people and said, "How long will you waver between two opinions? If the LORD is God, follow him; but if Baal is God, follow him."

But the people said nothing.

[22] Then Elijah said to them, "I am the only one of the LORD's prophets left, but Baal has four hundred and fifty prophets. [23] Get two bulls for us. Let them choose one for themselves, and let them cut it into pieces and put it on the wood but not set fire to it. I will prepare the other bull and put it on the wood but not set fire to it. [24] Then you call on the name of your god, and I will call on the name of the LORD. The god who answers by fire—he is God." Then all the people said, "What you say is good."

[25] Elijah said to the prophets of Baal, "Choose one of the bulls and prepare it first, since there are so many of you. Call on the name of your god, but do not light the fire." [26] So they took the bull given them and prepared it.

Then they called on the name of Baal from morning till noon. "O Baal, answer us!" they shouted. But there was no response; no one answered. And they danced around the altar they had made.

[27] At noon Elijah began to taunt them. "Shout louder!" he said. "Surely he is a god! Perhaps he is deep in thought, or busy, or traveling. Maybe he is sleeping and must be awakened." [28] So they shouted louder and slashed themselves with swords and spears, as was their custom, until their blood flowed. [29] Midday passed, and they continued their frantic prophesying until the time for the evening sacrifice. But there was no response, no one answered, no one paid attention.

[30] Then Elijah said to all the people, "Come here to me." They came to him, and he repaired the altar of the LORD, which was in ruins. [31] Elijah took twelve stones, one for each of the tribes descended from Jacob, to whom the word of the LORD had come, saying, "Your name shall be Israel." [32] With the stones he built an altar in the name of the LORD, and he dug a trench around it large enough to hold two seahs of seed. [33] He arranged the wood, cut the bull into pieces and laid it on the wood. Then he said to them, "Fill four large jars with water and pour it on the offering and on the wood."

[34] "Do it again," he said, and they did it again.

"Do it a third time," he ordered, and they did it the third time. [35] The water ran down around the altar and even filled the trench.

[36] At the time of sacrifice, the prophet Elijah stepped forward and prayed: "O LORD, God of Abraham, Isaac and Israel, let it be known today that you are God in Israel and that I am your servant and have done all these things at your command. [37] Answer me, O LORD, answer me, so these people will know that you, O LORD, are God, and that you are turning their hearts back again."

[38] Then the fire of the LORD fell and burned up the sacrifice, the wood, the stones and the soil, and also licked up the water in the trench.

[39] When all the people saw this, they fell prostrate and cried, "The LORD -he is God! The LORD -he is God!"

Proving God's Power:
Elijah Burns Baal

1 Kings 18:16-21

1. When Ahab wrongly accused Elijah of causing trouble, what did Elijah do (17-18)?

stayed quiet   agreed with Ahab, trying to turn an enemy into a friend

ran away   told Ahab the truth -- that the king caused trouble by rejecting God

2. Circle everything Elijah told Israel (21) when they were saying that they followed God, but also taking part in festivals to false gods?

It's OK. Worship all the gods you like.   Worship God one day and Baal the next.

How long will you waver between two opinions?   If the Lord is God, follow Him;

Mind Changers

1. Persevering to follow God may mean speaking hard truths. How would you answer?

(A) A friend feels bad because he stole candy from a store. Mark or write what you'd say.

___ It's no big deal; you'll feel better over time.

___ Stealing is wrong. You feel bad because you disobeyed God and broke the law. You won't feel better until you talk to the store owner and give the candy back.

___ _____

(B) A friend is upset because she yelled at her mom. Mark or write what you'd say.

___ God wants us to honor our parents. You need to tell her that you're sorry.

___ Just stay at my house awhile until she gets over it.

___ _____

Lesson 3 Memory Verse
1 Kings 18:37

Answer me, O Lord, answer me, so these people will know that you, O Lord, are God, and that you are turning their hearts back again.

Proving God's Power:
Elijah Burns Baal

1 Kings 18:22-27

1. How many of the Lord's prophets did Elijah say were left (22)? _____

2. How many prophets of Baal were there (22)? _____

3. Color the right number of each block to get a picture of how Elijah was outnumbered.

Lord's Prophets = 1   Baal's Prophets = 450

100s   10s   5s   1s   100s   10s   5s   1s

4. Did Elijah ever stop speaking the truth because he was outnumbered?   YES   NO

5. It's important to be able to tell the one true God from false gods. Circle why no fire came to burn the sacrifice on the altar to Baal (26-27).

Prophets didn't call loudly enough.   Baal wasn't real and had no power.

It wasn't the right time of day.   Prophets didn't know the right dance steps.

Baal was traveling.   Baal was sleeping.

Mind Changers

1. Elijah said and did things that pleased God even when he was outnumbered. What would you say if…

(A) your 5 friends wanted to see a movie that nobody's parents allowed?

___ "Our parents won't let us see this. We need to pick something else."

___ "They'll never find out. We can sneak in."

___ _____

(B) you were supposed to go with 3 friends to church, but they wanted to go shopping?

___ "Hey, shopping sounds fun. Maybe we can go to church twice next week."

___ "It's Sunday, guys, we have to worship God. It's His holy day."

___ _____

2. How well do you know the one true God? Circle only things you think God would do.

answer a prayer for a friend to get well   tell you to steal a bike for someone

bless a family with a new baby   tell you to take dinner to a sick person

send His Son to save the world from sin   tell you to lie so friends don't get in trouble

Put the memory verse phrases in correct order. Write 1 by the first, 2 by the second, etc.

___ so these people will know that you, O Lord, are God,
___ Answer me, O Lord, answer me,
___ back again. 1 Kings 18:37
___ and that you are turning their hearts

Lesson 3

Proving God's Power:
Elijah Burns Baal

1 Kings 18:27-36

1. The Baal prophets did crazy things to get their god to send fire. Elijah knew what the true God expected from His followers. Mark what Elijah did to ask God to send fire. (36)

___ yelled at God   ___ danced a special dance   ___ cut himself   ___ prayed

You're Wonderful! God's Word says that you are wonderfully made and that all His works are wonderful. (Psalm 139:14) God created your body. So you should never do anything to hurt it. God never wants you to harm yourself like the Baal prophets. You're much too special to Him!

2. Persevering means obeying God and doing hard work for Him. Circle all the work Elijah did (30-33).

repaired the altar of the Lord   moved 12 stones   dug a trench   built houses

arranged wood   went fishing   cut up a bull and laid pieces on wood

3. Why do you think Elijah asked the people to pour water on the wood and didn't do it himself (33)? Mark all that you think are right.

___ Elijah was lazy.   ___ Elijah was tired.

___ Elijah didn't want the people to think he was playing a trick on them.

Mind Changers

1. Do you know what God expects from His followers? Circle all the things that make the next sentence true. **God is happy with me when I...**

pray   fight with a brother or sister   read my Bible   pout or whine

help others   go to church   sing to Him   obey Him

2. Write one thing that you will do to please God today. _____

3. Sometimes persevering means doing hard work. Circle ways below that you have worked hard to persevere or write in other things.

washing dishes   working on difficult homework or a paper

helping your family clean or do laundry   helping with yard work

_____   _____

Cross out wrong words in your memory verse.
Write correct words above.

Answer me, O Lord, call me, so these pineapples will know that you, O

Lord, are busy, and that you are painting their hearts red again.

1 Kings 18:37

Lesson 3

Day 4

Proving God's Power:
Elijah Burns Baal

1 Kings 18:36-39

1. Who commanded Elijah to build an altar and expect fire to come (36)? Circle one.

Ahab   Baal   God   Joshua   Jezebel

2. Years earlier, God had told Israel the special times He wanted their sacrifices. Finish the first part of verse 36, showing that Elijah was careful about when he worshipped God.

At the _____ ___ _____, the prophet Elijah stepped forward and prayed:

3. Circle everything Elijah wanted the people to know (36-37).

God was the only God in Israel   Elijah was God's servant   Elijah had lots of money

Elijah liked fireworks   God was turning the people to Him   Elijah obeyed God

4. Mark everything that happened because Elijah persevered.

__ fire fell   __ the sacrifice burned   __ wood burned

__ stones burned   __ soil burned   __ they roasted marshmallows

__ the people saw that the Lord was really the one true God and fell to worship Him

Mind Changers

1. To persevere, Elijah had to obey God. Mark the commands of God that you obey.

___ 1 Have no other Gods before me. ___ 2 Honor your father and mother.

___ 3 Don't make a statue to worship. ___ 4 Only use God's Name in holy ways.

___ 5 Keep a holy Sunday.   ___ 6 Do not kill anyone.

___ 7 Do not steal.   ___ 8 Do not take another person's husband or wife.

___ 9 Do not lie   .   ___ 10 Do not be jealous of others' things.

2. Which commands in question 1 do you need to do a better job keeping? _____

3. People who persevere for God want others to know who He is and what He does. Write the names of 3 people you can tell about God.

_____   _____   _____

4. For each name you wrote, write one thing you want to tell that person about God.

_____   _____   _____

Write missing words to finish your memory verse.

Answer me, O _____, _____ me, so these people will _____ that

you, O Lord, are _____, and that you are turning their _____ back again.
1 Kings 18:____

Lesson 3

Proving God's Power:
Elijah Burns Baal

What did you learn from Elijah?

Read back over your answers this week. Then put an **X** in the ☐ by ideas that were new to you or that made you think differently about how a person who perseveres acts.

People who persevere in doing God's work...

☐ 1. keep speaking God's truth, even when it's not popular.

☐ 2. trust God's power, even when outnumbered.

☐ 3. can always tell the one true God from false gods.

☐ 4. know what God expects of His followers.

☐ 5. keep working hard to do what God wants.

☐ 6. do God's work God's way, following His commands.

☐ 7. want others to know that only God is God.

☐ 8. cause others to worship God as their God.

Put an **X** in this ☐ if you can say 1 Kings 18:37 from memory.

Bible Verses for Lesson 4

Nehemiah 1:11–2:20

(Nehemiah was sad when he heard that God's special city, Jerusalem, had been burned down. He knew God wanted him to rebuild it, but Nehemiah had a high position under King Artaxerxes. Would the king let Nehemiah go to do the work?)

[11] O LORD, let your ear be attentive to the prayer of this your servant and to the prayer of your servants who delight in revering your name. Give your servant success today by granting him favor in the presence of this man."

I was cupbearer to the king.

2 [1] In the month of Nisan in the twentieth year of King Artaxerxes, when wine was brought for him, I took the wine and gave it to the king. I had not been sad in his presence before; [2] so the king asked me, "Why does your face look so sad when you are not ill? This can be nothing but sadness of heart."

I was very much afraid, [3] but I said to the king, "May the king live forever! Why should my face not look sad when the city where my fathers are buried lies in ruins, and its gates have been destroyed by fire?"

[4] The king said to me, "What is it you want?"

Then I prayed to the God of heaven, [5] and I answered the king, "If it pleases the king and if your servant has found favor in his sight, let him send me to the city in Judah where my fathers are buried so that I can rebuild it." [6] Then the king, with the queen sitting beside him, asked me, "How long will your journey take, and when will you get back?" It pleased the king to send me; so I set a time.

[7] I also said to him, "If it pleases the king, may I have letters to the governors of Trans-Euphrates, so that they will provide me safe-conduct until I arrive in Judah? [8] And may I have a letter to Asaph, keeper of the king's forest, so he will give me timber to make beams for the gates of the citadel by the temple and for the city wall and for the residence I will occupy?" And because the gracious hand of my God was upon me, the king granted my requests. [9] So I went to the governors of Trans-Euphrates and gave them the king's letters. The king had also sent army officers and cavalry with me.

[10] When Sanballat the Horonite and Tobiah the Ammonite official heard about this, they were very much disturbed that someone had come to promote the welfare of the Israelites.

[11] I went to Jerusalem, and after staying there three days [12] I set out during the night with a few men. I had not told anyone what my God had put in my heart to do for Jerusalem.

There were no mounts with me except the one I was riding on.

[13] By night I went out through the Valley Gate toward the Jackal Well and the Dung Gate, examining the walls of Jerusalem, which had been broken down, and its gates, which had been destroyed by fire. [14] Then I moved on toward the Fountain Gate and the King's Pool, but there was not enough room for my mount to get through; [15] so I went up the valley by night, examining the wall. Finally, I turned back and reentered through the Valley Gate. [16] The officials did not know where I had gone or what I was doing, because as yet I had said nothing to the Jews or the priests or nobles or officials or any others who would be doing the work.

[17] Then I said to them, "You see the trouble we are in: Jerusalem lies in ruins, and its gates have been burned with fire. Come, let us rebuild the wall of Jerusalem, and we will no longer be in disgrace." [18] I also told them about the gracious hand of my God upon me and what the king had said to me.

They replied, "Let us start rebuilding." So they began this good work.

[19] But when Sanballat the Horonite, Tobiah the Ammonite official and Geshem the Arab heard about it, they mocked and ridiculed us. "What is this you are doing?" they asked. "Are you rebelling against the king?"

[20] I answered them by saying, "The God of heaven will give us success. We his servants will start rebuilding, but as for you, you have no share in Jerusalem or any claim or historic right to it."

Building for God:
Nehemiah Begins the Wall

Nehemiah 1:11–2:6

1. Write a word that tells the first thing Nehemiah did to begin the rebuilding work (11).

"O Lord, let your ear be attentive to the _____ of this your servant and to the prayer of the servants who delight in revering your name."

2. What did Nehemiah do even in the middle of talking to the king (2:4)?

The king said to me, "What is it you want?" Then I _____ to the God of heaven,

3. Knowing who we should pray to is as important as remembering to pray at all. Circle the One to whom Nehemiah prayed (4).

the king   God of heaven   a manmade statue   lots of different gods

4. It's normal to be nervous doing new, big things. Did Nehemiah's fear stop him from asking the king if he could go do God's work (2-3)? Circle one.   YES   NO

5. Write words from the end of verse 6 showing that Nehemiah's perseverance paid off.

It pleased the king to _____ _____; so I _____ a time.

Mind Changers

1. Underline the first thing you think of doing when you have a big job to do. Circle what you think God wants you to do first.

get other people to help with the work   make a plan and schedule

hide to avoid doing the work   pray

2. We can say "arrow prayers" to ask God's help in the middle of problems. For the situation written below each arrow, write a short prayer INSIDE the arrow.

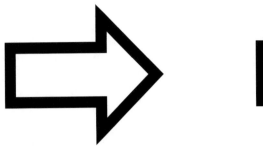 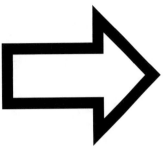

A friend asks why you believe in Jesus.   You must pick the right gift for a sick friend.

3. We often need to ignore fear and do the next right thing. Circle what you would do.

(A) What if you see your teacher, whom your mom has never met, in the grocery store?

pretend not to see the teacher since you're shy   run to another place in the store

be polite and respectful; introduce them to each other

(B) What if you're tired of working on a homework project that is due tomorrow?

find someone else to finish it   pray for God's help and energy, and finish the work

find something you can copy and turn in from the internet

Lesson 4 Memory Verse
Nehemiah 2:20 (part 1 only)

I answered them by saying, "The God of heaven will give us success."

Building for God:
Nehemiah Begins the Wall

Nehemiah 2:7-12

1. In the end of verse 8, what did Nehemiah say caused the king to grant his requests?

And because the _____ _____ _____ _____ _____
was upon me, the king granted my requests.

2. In the end of verse 9, what extra blessing did Nehemiah get that he did not request?

The king had also sent _____ _____ and _____ with me.

3. Was Sanballat glad to hear Nehemiah was rebuilding Jerusalem (10)?   YES   NO

4. Who gave Nehemiah the plan to rebuild the walls of Jerusalem (12)? Circle one.

The king   Sanballat   Tobiah   God   Nehemiah's mom

Mind Changers

1. Every blessing is from God. For what do you need to thank Him for right now?

_____   _____   _____

2.   Write down a blessing that you didn't ask for, but God gave you anyway. Thank Him.

_____

3. Nehemiah followed God's plan. Circle good ways that you can find out God's plan for how He wants you to do things.

talk to a parent who knows Jesus   read your Bible   pray

talk to a pastor   talk to a Christian friend   guess

What Can God Do to Help Us?

Circle the highest number in each row and write the word above it on the line at the side. Find out what God is able to do to help us; read top to bottom.

turkey	little	some	cat	more	
5	15	0	3	25	_____

over	around	than	into	under	
2	12	20	5	7	_____

all	in	much	none	peace	
18	0	4	10	3	_____

me	we	you	I	us	
14	33	22	11	6	_____

run	hit	fly	ask	sing	
3	19	17	21	1	_____

and	but	or	if	on	
0	2	8	1	6	_____

question	imagine	wonder	ponder	think	
20	100	10	40	30	_____

Cross out wrong words in your memory verse.
Write correct words above.

I fooled them by saying, "The clouds of heaven will give us popcorn."
Nehemiah 2:20 (part 1 only)

Lesson 4

Day 3

Building for God:
Nehemiah Begins the Wall

Nehemiah 2:13-18

1. Mark the box by the wise, practical step Nehemiah took before rebuilding (13).

☐ found the guys who broke the walls   ☐ examined the walls   ☐ worked out

2. Why do you think Nehemiah looked at the walls before he began to build?

to find buried treasure   to see how big the job was   he wanted fresh air

3. How did Nehemiah encourage the people who would help him work (18)?

I also told them about the gracious _____ of my _____ upon me and what the king had said to me.

Mind Changers

1. Nehemiah looked at the broken wall to see how much work there was. How would you "research the size of the project" for these jobs?

(A) You are going to clean up a sick neighbor's yard. Circle the best way to "research."

rent a helicopter to fly over   walk the yard to see bags needed for leaves or trash

(B) You are going to shovel snow from a neighbor's driveway. How would you research?

check how deep the snow is with your shovel   count snowflakes

Circle the right word in each pair
in your memory verse – Nehemiah 2:20 (part 1 only).

I (called , answered) them by saying, "The God of (heaven , Texas) will give us success."

Lesson 4

Day 4

Building for God:
Nehemiah Begins the Wall

Nehemiah 2:18–20

1. When Nehemiah told the workers God was with them, what did they want to do (18)?

take a nap   start rebuilding   bake brownies   feed fish

2. When Sanballat, Tobiah and Gesham heard of the rebuilding, what did they do (19)?

roasted marshmallows to celebrate   planned a party   mocked

3. Who did Nehemiah trust to give him success (20)?   Tobiah   God of heaven

Mind Changers

1. Circle groups you would be willing to build up by telling them that God is with them.

church group serving in the community   kids cleaning up an area park

your church choir or praise band   local firefighters

2. Circle ways you can show God you trust Him like Nehemiah.

read your Bible and try to live as it says   pray for God to bless your work for Him

ask Jesus to be your Savior (Read pages 93 & 94 if you're not sure what that means.)

Write missing words to finish your memory verse.

I _____ them by _____, "The _____ of heaven will _____

us _____" Nehemiah 2: ____ (part 1 only)

Building for God:
Nehemiah Begins the Wall

What did you learn from Nehemiah starting the wall?

Read back over your answers this week. Then put an **X** in the ☐ by ideas that were new to you or that made you think differently about how a person who perseveres acts.

People who persevere in doing God's work...

☐ 1. know prayer is the first step in persevering.

☐ 2. don't let fear keep them from saying or doing the next right thing.

☐ 3. know God is the source of success.

☐ 4. follow plans directed by God.

☐ 5. research the size of their project.

☐ 6. tell others the good things God's doing.

☐ 7. motivate others to join God's plans.

☐ 8. trust God for success.

Put an **X** in this ☐ if you can say part 1 of Nehemiah 2:20 from memory.

Bible Verses for Lesson 5

Selected verses from Nehemiah – chapters 4, 5, & 6

(As Jerusalem's wall grew stronger, so did efforts by Nehemiah's enemies to destroy him and stop the project! Would the people finish?)

4 ^{1} When Sanballat heard that we were rebuilding the wall, he became angry and was greatly incensed. He ridiculed the Jews, **(Nehemiah prayed.)**

^{4} Hear us, O our God, for we are despised. Turn their insults back on their own heads. Give them over as plunder in a land of captivity. ^{5} Do not cover up their guilt or blot out their sins from your sight, for they have thrown insults in the face of the builders. ^{6} So we rebuilt the wall till all of it reached half its height, for the people worked with all their heart. ^{7} But when Sanballat, Tobiah, the Arabs, the Ammonites and the men of Ashdod heard that the repairs to Jerusalem's walls had gone ahead and that the gaps were being closed, they were very angry. ^{8} They all plotted together to come and fight against Jerusalem and stir up trouble against it. ^{9} But we prayed to our God and posted a guard day and night to meet this threat.

^{11} Also our enemies said, "Before they know it or see us, we will be right there among them and will kill them and put an end to the work." ^{13} Therefore I stationed some of the people behind the lowest points of the wall at the exposed places, posting them by families, with their swords, spears and bows. ^{14} After I looked things over, I stood up and said to the nobles, the officials and the rest of the people, "Don't be afraid of them. Remember the LORD, who is great and awesome, and fight for your brothers, your sons and your daughters, your wives and your homes."

^{15} When our enemies heard that we were aware of their plot and that God had frustrated it, we all returned to the wall, each to his own work. ^{16} From that day on, half of my men did the work, while the other half were equipped with spears, shields, bows and armor. The officers posted themselves behind all the people of Judah ^{17} who were building the wall. Those who carried materials did their work with one hand and held a weapon in the other, ^{18} and each of the builders wore his sword at his side as he worked. But the man who sounded the trumpet stayed with me.

^{19} Then I said to the nobles, the officials and the rest of the people, "The work is extensive and spread out, and we are widely separated from each other along the wall. ^{20} Wherever you hear the sound of the trumpet, join us there. Our God will fight for us!"

5 ^{14} Moreover, from the twentieth year of King Artaxerxes, when I was appointed to be their governor in the land of Judah, until his thirty-second year—twelve years—neither I nor my brothers ate the food allotted to the governor. ^{15} But the earlier governors—those preceding me—placed a heavy burden on the people and took forty shekels of silver from them in addition to food and wine. Their assistants also lorded it over the people. But out of reverence for God I did not act like that. ^{16} Instead, I devoted myself to the work on this wall. All my men were assembled there for the work; we did not acquire any land. ^{17} Furthermore, a hundred and fifty Jews and officials ate at my table, as well as those who came to us from the surrounding nations.

6 ^{2} Sanballat and Geshem sent me this message: "Come, let us meet together in one of the villages on the plain of Ono." But they were scheming to harm me; ^{3} so I sent messengers to them with this reply: "I am carrying on a great project and cannot go down. Why should the work stop while I leave it and go down to you?" ^{4} Four times they sent me the same message, and each time I gave them the same answer. ^{5} Then, the fifth time, Sanballat sent his aide to me with the same message, and in his hand was an unsealed letter ^{6} in which was written:

"It is reported among the nations—and Geshem says it is true—that you and the Jews are plotting to revolt, and therefore you are building the wall. Moreover, according to these reports you are about to become their king ^{7} and have even appointed prophets to make this proclamation about you in Jerusalem: 'There is a king in Judah!' Now this report will get back to the king; so come, let us confer together."

^{8} I sent him this reply: "Nothing like what you are saying is happening; you are just making it up out of your head." ^{9} They were all trying to frighten us, thinking, "Their hands will get too weak for the work, and it will not be completed."

But I prayed, "Now strengthen my hands."

^{10} One day I went to the house of Shemaiah son of Delaiah, the son of Mehetabel, who was shut in at his home. He said, "Let us meet in the house of God, inside the temple, and let us close the temple doors, because men are coming to kill you—by night they are coming to kill you."

^{11} But I said, "Should a man like me run away? Or should one like me go into the temple to save his life? I will not go!" ^{13} He had been hired to intimidate me so that I would commit a sin by doing this, and then they would give me a bad name to discredit me.

^{15} So the wall was completed on the twenty-fifth of Elul, in fifty-two days. ^{16} When all our enemies heard about this, all the surrounding nations were afraid and lost their self-confidence, because they realized that this work had been done with the help of our God.

Lesson 5

Overcoming the Opposition
Nehemiah Completes the Wall

Nehemiah 4:1-9

1. After Sanballat ridiculed the Jews, what did Nehemiah do (4)? Circle one.

ran and hid   called for more soldiers   prayed, "Hear us, O our God…"

2. After Sanballat plotted to fight against Jerusalem, what did Nehemiah do? (9)

made fun of Sanballat's name   prayed   quit working

3. Do you think Nehemiah ever took days off from praying?

                    YES   NO

4. Write words from the first part of verse 6 showing what was happening.

So we _____ the _____ till all of it reached half its height,

5. Write words from verse 6 showing why Nehemiah said they were able to build well.

for the people _____ with all their _____ .

49

Mind Changers

1. God wants us to keep praying! Circle the longest time you might have to pray about:

(A) a school science project   minutes   hours days   weeks years

(B) a loved one believing in Jesus   minutes   hours days   weeks years

2. What will you start praying about consistently? _____

3. Circle what "working with all your heart" means.

running hard   putting all your energy and effort into the work   lifting weights

4. Circle all words that mean the <u>opposite</u> of "working with all your heart."

lazy   energetic   delaying   sleeping

5. God's Word says, "Whatever you do, work at it with all your heart, as working for the Lord, not for men." (Colossians 3:23) Write what you would do differently if:

(A) you had to turn schoolwork in to God _____

(B) you had to clean your room for God's inspection _____

Lesson 5 Memory Verse
Nehemiah 4:6

So we rebuilt the wall till all of it reached half its height, for the people
worked with all their heart.

Overcoming the Opposition
Nehemiah Completes the Wall

Nehemiah 4:7–15

1. Nehemiah always added practical action to his prayers. Circle all he did after Sanballat plotted with others to fight against Jerusalem (9).

went into panic   prayed   posted a guard   had a parade

2. When the enemies threatened to kill the workers, what did Nehemiah do (13)?

Therefore I _____ some of the people behind the lowest points of the wall at the exposed places, posting them by families, with their swords, spears and bows.

3. Write what Nehemiah said to encourage the people to have faith in God, not fear (14).

"Don't be _____ of them. Remember the _____, who is great and _____;

4. When the workers trusted in God, what did God do (15)? Circle one.

left them to be killed   frustrated the enemy plot   made them weak

---

What About praying for Our Enemies? Jesus did tell us to pray for our enemies. However, because Sanballat and the other enemies were against the Jews (God's special people), they had set themselves up against God. God had already judged them. Their days were numbered. God does want us to pray for those who attack us, but when someone attacks our holy God or His people, we are to stand up for them!

Mind Changers

1. Draw lines between the prayers below and the matching practical actions.

PRAY TO: PRACTICAL ACTION

get good grades   exercise and eat with good nutrition

win an essay contest   study

have a healthy body   practice your recital piece

perform well in your recital   take your time writing an excellent essay

2. What do you need to pray about today? _____

3. What practical action will you add to that prayer? _____

Put the memory verse phrases in correct order.
Write 1 by the first, 2 by the second, etc.
___ with all their heart. Nehemiah 4:6
___ till all of it reached half its height,
___ So we rebuilt the wall
___ for the people worked

Lesson 5   Day 3
Overcoming the Opposition
Nehemiah Completes the Wall

Nehemiah 4:16-20 & 5:14-17

1. Write words showing Nehemiah planned and prepared to guard against attacks (16).

From that day on, half of my men did the _____ ,
while the other half were equipped with spears, shields, _____ and armor.

2. What was Nehemiah's plan to organize the workers to defend an attack (20)?

Wherever you hear the sound of the _____ , join us there. Our God will fight for us!"

3. Carefully read 5:14-17. Mark T (true) or F (false) by each statement about how Nehemiah treated the people. Nehemiah:

___ was appointed governor

___ ate up all the food allotted to the governor

___ placed a heavy burden on the people

___ out of reverence for God, did not burden the people

___ devoted himself to work on the wall

___ fed 150 Jews and officials at his table

___ stole land from the people

Mind Changers

1. Mark boxes by all those who might be your enemies. If you're trying your best to follow God, an enemy might be someone who:

☐ draws you into gossip   ☐ tries to get you to lie for him

☐ begs you to go to a movie instead of church   ☐ teases you for praying at lunch

2. Circle all you should do in order to prepare for these "enemy attacks."

pray daily for wisdom   stock up on rubber bands to shoot enemies

be mean to people first   read the Bible so you'll know what God expects of you

learn to beat people up   memorize verses so you'll always have a godly response

3. Circle ways you can be kind to those who work and play with you.

share games and toys   push kids down who don't do things your way

offer to pray for others   include others when you play or go fun places

be a kind host to visitors   invite friends to church with you

Color the box by the verse that is written right.

☐ So we rebuilt the wall till all of it reached half its height, for the workers worked with all their heart. Nehemiah 4:16

☐ So we built the wall till all of it reached half its length, for the people worked with all their heart. Nehemiah 4:6

☐ So we rebuilt the wall till all of it reached half its height, for the people worked with all their heart. Nehemiah 4:6

Lesson 5   Day 4
Overcoming the Opposition
Nehemiah Completes the Wall

Nehemiah 6:2-16

1. Complete phrases from verses 2-13 showing that Sanballat was trying to hurt Nehemiah and stop the work.

But they were scheming to _____ me; (2)

They were all trying to _____ us, thinking, "Their hands will get too weak

for the _____, and it will not be _____." (9)

He had been hired to _____ me so that I would commit a _____ by doing this, and then they would give me a bad name and discredit me. (13)

2. Write T (true) or F (false) as to how Nehemiah responded (3-11).

___ Nehemiah told Sanballat he could not stop the work to meet him.

___ Nehemiah sent Sanballat e-mails saying "Leave me alone."

___ Nehemiah said, "Nothing like what you are saying is happening;"

___ Nehemiah prayed.

___ Nehemiah asked, "Or should one like me go into the temple to save his life?"

3. Circle all the ways Nehemiah's building project brought glory to God (15-16).

It was completed in 52 days.   The people made Nehemiah King.

Surrounding enemies were afraid.   Enemies lost self-confidence.

Nehemiah made fun of the enemies. Everyone realized God helped do the work.

Mind Changers

1. Draw lines to match an "attack" you might hear with a godly response.

ATTACK   GODLY RESPONSE

Sending orphans money can't make a difference.   The prayer of a righteous man is
                                                    powerful and effective.

Do you think God really hears prayers?   All scripture is God-breathed and
                                                    is useful for teaching, rebuking,
                                                    correcting and training in
                                                    righteousness,

The Bible isn't for today.   God says to care for orphans.

2. Write names of people who might be your enemies.

_____   _____   _____

3. Write 1 thing you can pray for each one. (Assume their hearts are not set against God).

_____   _____   _____

📖 Write in what's missing to finish your memory verse.

So we _____ the _____ till all of it reached _____ its height,

for the people _____ with _____ their heart.

Nehemiah __ : ___

Overcoming the Opposition
Nehemiah Completes the Wall

What did you learn from Nehemiah finishing the wall?

Read back over your answers this week. Then put an **X** in the □ by ideas that were new to you or that made you think differently about how a person who perseveres acts.

People who persevere in doing God's work...

□ 1. pray all the way through problems.

□ 2. work with all their heart.

□ 3. add practical action to prayer.

□ 4. choose faith in God over fear.

□ 5. plan and prepare for enemy attacks.

□ 6. are kind to those with whom they work or play.

□ 7. watch for enemies' evil tricks and respond with prayer and wisdom.

□ 8. ultimately bring glory to God.

Put an **X** in this □ if you can say Nehemiah 4:6 from memory.

Bible Verses for Lesson 6
John 9:11–38

(When Jesus heals a blind man, the people and authorities press the man to change his story and talk badly of Jesus. How will he handle the pressure?)

[11]He replied, "The man they call Jesus made some mud and put it on my eyes. He told me to go to Siloam and wash. So I went and washed, and then I could see." [12]"Where is this man?" they asked him. "I don't know," he said.

[13]They brought to the Pharisees the man who had been blind. [14]Now the day on which Jesus had made the mud and opened the man's eyes was a Sabbath. [15]Therefore the Pharisees also asked him how he had received his sight. "He put mud on my eyes," the man replied, "and I washed, and now I see."

[16]Some of the Pharisees said, "This man is not from God, for he does not keep the Sabbath." But others asked, "How can a sinner do such miraculous signs?" So they were divided. [17]Finally they turned again to the blind man, "What have you to say about him? It was your eyes he opened." The man replied, "He is a prophet."

[18]The Jews still did not believe that he had been blind and had received his sight until they sent for the man's parents. [19]"Is this your son?" they asked. "Is this the one you say was born blind? How is it that now he can see?"

[20]"We know he is our son," the parents answered, "and we know he was born blind. [21]But how he can see now, or who opened his eyes, we don't know. Ask him. He is of age; he will speak for himself." [22]His parents said this because they were afraid of the Jews, for already the Jews had decided that anyone who acknowledged that Jesus was the Christ would be put out of the synagogue. [23]That was why his parents said, "He is of age; ask him."

[24]A second time they summoned the man who had been blind. "Give glory to God," they said. "We know this man is a sinner." [25]He replied, "Whether he is a sinner or not, I don't know. One thing I do know. I was blind but now I see!" [26]Then they asked him, "What did he do to you? How did he open your eyes?" [27]He answered, "I have told you already and you did not listen. Why do you want to hear it again? Do you want to become his disciples, too?"

[28]Then they hurled insults at him and said, "You are this fellow's disciple! We are disciples of Moses! [29]We know that God spoke to Moses, but as for this fellow, we don't even know where he comes from."

³⁰The man answered, "Now that is remarkable! You don't know where he comes from, yet he opened my eyes. ³¹We know that God does not listen to sinners. He listens to the godly man who does his will. ³²Nobody has ever heard of opening the eyes of a man born blind. ³³If this man were not from God, he could do nothing."

³⁴To this they replied, "You were steeped in sin at birth; how dare you lecture us!" And they threw him out.

³⁵Jesus heard that they had thrown him out, and when he found him, he said, "Do you believe in the Son of Man?"

³⁶"Who is he, sir?" the man asked. "Tell me so that I may believe in him."

³⁷Jesus said, "You have now seen him; in fact, he is the one speaking with you."

³⁸Then the man said, "Lord, I believe," and he worshiped him.

Lesson 6

Day 1

Standing for Truth:
A Blind Man Boasts of Jesus

John 9:11-15

1. What did the man tell people who asked how he could see (11)? Circle T or F.

T	F	Jesus made mud and put it on my shoes.
T	F	Jesus made mud and put it on my eyes.
T	F	Jesus told me to go to Siloam and wash.
T	F	So I went to take a nap and when I woke up I could see.
T	F	So I went and washed, and then I could see.

2. Circle the right answer below. The blind man was blessed because…

he did what he felt like doing.   he obeyed Jesus' words exactly.

3. Did fear of being made fun of stop the man from telling neighbors
the truth of how Jesus healed Him?   YES   NO

4. What did the man tell the Pharisees who asked how he could see (15)? Circle T or F.

T	F	He put mud on my ears.	T	F	He put mud on my eyes.
T	F	He made me count to 10.	T	F	I washed, and now I see.

Why Fear Pharisees? Religious leaders, called Pharisees, held the most power over the Jews. Pharisees were much more worried about forcing people to keep their religious laws than about loving people like Jesus did. They rejected Jesus – and anyone else who thought He was good or from God. They had power to kick Jews out of the synagogue -- the required place of worship and the center of community life for Jews!

5. Did fear of the Pharisees keep the man from telling them the
truth of how Jesus healed Him?   YES   NO

60

Mind Changers

1. People who persevere obey Jesus' words exactly. Circle what you would do:

(A) God's Word says, "You shall not steal," but a friend wants you to distract a clerk in a store so he can sneak out of the door with a new baseball glove and not pay.

Tell him stealing is a sin and illegal.   Get the clerk away from the door.

(B) God's Word says, "You shall not misuse the name of the Lord your God," but some kids want you to swear using God's name to show you're like the "popular kids."

Misuse God's name just this once.   Tell them God's name is holy, not a curse.

2. What's your answer if someone asks you, "What has Jesus done for you?"

_____

Lesson 6 Memory Verse
John 9:35

Jesus heard that they had thrown him out, and when he found him, he said,

"Do you believe in the Son of Man?"

Lesson 6

Day 2

Standing for Truth:
A Blind Man Boasts of Jesus

John 9:16-24

1. Circle what the Pharisees thought (16). Jesus is: not from God.   a prophet.

2. Circle why the Pharisees thought that.

He does not keep the Sabbath.   He does not wear the right clothes.

3. Did the man change his story when the Pharisees asked him again (17)? Circle one.

Yes. He said Jesus didn't really make him see.   No. He said Jesus was a prophet.

Just a Prophet? Jesus was much more than a prophet. He was and is God! However, the man had not figured this out yet. He only knew that Jesus was sent by God to do God's work. That's why he called Jesus a prophet even though the Pharisees disagreed. Here's what's funny. The questions the Pharisees asked (trying to make the man change his story about Jesus) really helped him know for sure that Jesus was sent by God!

4. Circle why the man's parents were quiet about how their son got his sight (22).

They were sick and had lost their voices.   They were afraid.   They were sleepy.

5. Write what may have happened to anyone who said that Jesus was the Christ. They:

"would be _____ _____ of the synagogue."

6. Did the man face the same penalty?   YES   NO

7. "Give glory to God" was the Pharisees' way of saying, "Now tell the truth." What else did they say to push the man to change his story (24)?

"We know this man is a _____."

Mind Changers

1. Imagine that your Dad has 2 job offers in different cities and your family is praying about which to take. One day you read in your Bible "He led them by a straight way to a city where they could settle." (Psalm 107:7) You are excited that God "spoke" to you to encourage you and you tell a friend. The friend says, "That's just a coincidence." Circle what you would say.

No way. God knows what I am concerned about. He sent me a special message to let me know He's with me!

Yeah, you're probably right.

2. Imagine you have to write a paper on the most important person in your life. God is most important to you so you feel you should write about Him, but you wonder if kids will make fun of you. You pray and read in your Bible "Then the Lord said to Moses, "'Write down these words…'" (Exodus 34:27) Circle what you would do next.

Think it's just coincidence to read something on writing after praying about writing.

Get busy writing about God being most important to you.

Color the box by the verse that is written right.

☐ Jesus saw that they had thrown him a fish, and when he found him, he said, "Do you believe in the Son of Man?" John 9:35

☐ Jesus heard that they had thrown him out, and when he caught him, he said, "Do you know the Son of Man?" Jane 9:30

☐ Jesus heard that they had thrown him out, and when he found him, he said, "Do you believe in the Son of Man?" John 9:35

Lesson 6

Day 3

Standing for Truth:
A Blind Man Boasts of Jesus

John 9:15-34

1. In 15, 17, 24 & 26, how many times did the Pharisees question the man?

1 time   2 times   3 times   4 times   5 times

2. Write words telling what the man finally invited the Pharisees to do (27).

Do you _____ to _____ His disciples, too?

3. The Pharisees had already turned their hearts against Jesus. Circle what they did. (28)

They hurled insults.   They enthusiastically said, "Yes!"

They threw onions at the man.   They claimed to be Moses' disciples.

4. Draw lines from each phrase to show who said these things (24-34).

This man is a sinner.   I was blind, but now I see!   We don't know where
                                                                 he comes from.

Man born blind & healed   **Pharisees**

If this man were not from God   We are Moses' disciples!
he could do nothing.

                                         We know God doesn't listen to sinners.
Do you want to become
his disciples, too?   How dare you lecture us!

5. Circle who boldly shared what they knew of God.   the man   Pharisees

Mind Changers

1. If you're in a situation where people keep asking you questions about Jesus so you'll say that He is not God, how many times are you willing to say He is God?

1 time   2 times   3 times   4 times   as many times as it takes

2. Who should you invite to believe in Jesus? _____

3. Write possible reasons that person has not yet asked Jesus to be his or her Savior?

_____

4. How can you answer his or her question or concern? (See pages 93 & 94 for help.)

_____

5. Circle what you know about God and would be willing to tell someone else.

Jesus is God.   God created the world.   God holds all things together.

God is always right.   Jesus saved us from sin.   God will punish all who reject Him.

God's Word is true.   God speaks in the Bible.   God wants us all to believe in Him.

6. Write the name of one person with whom you'll share one of these truths <u>and do it</u>.

_____

Circle the right word in each pair in your memory verse – John 9:35.

Jesus heard that (Peter Pan , they) had thrown (him , Humpty-Dumpty) out,

and when he (found , saw) him, he said, "Do you believe in the Son of Man?"

Standing for Truth:
A Blind Man Boasts of Jesus

John 9:35-38

1. We know Jesus listened to see how the man was doing (35) because "Jesus _____ that they had thrown him out,"

We know Jesus looked for the man to help him because "when he _____ him, he said, 'Do you believe in the Son of Man?' "

Who is the Son of Man? Jesus often called Himself the "Son of Man." It meant He was fully human, but not only human. "Son of Man" refers to God come to earth to rule here with authority, glory and all power. Since that hasn't happened yet, we know that Jesus will someday appear back on earth and rule in power. What an exciting time that will be!

2. Write words showing the man was willing to believe in Jesus not as just a prophet, but as his God (36)?

"Who is he, sir?" the man asked. " _____ me so that I may _____ in him."

3. Write words showing the man did believe when Jesus told him He was God (37-38)?

Then the man said, "_____, I _____," and he worshiped Him.

4. Circle blessings the man got when he boasted of Jesus and persevered to tell the truth.

a new car   Jesus looked for and found him   personal meeting with Jesus

strong faith   knowledge of Jesus as Son of Man   chance to worship Jesus

a trophy   Jesus revealed Himself in a new way

Mind Changers

1. Write something new that you have learned about Jesus because you have persevered in this Bible study.

_____

2. If you already chose to accept Jesus as your personal God, write about that time here.

_____

3. If you want to make that choice today, see pages 93 & 94 for the whole story. Write today's date here if you make that decision (and tell an adult). _____

4. Worshipping God means praising Him for who He is, what you know of His character. Circle everything you know for sure of God's character below; write in more if you like.

holy	knows everything	loving	perfect	always right
judge	slow to anger	merciful	Creator	Provider
powerful	only source of peace	Savior	unchanging	King of Kings

_____

📖 Write in what's missing to finish your memory verse.

_____ heard that they had _____him out, and when he _____

him, he said, "Do _____ believe in the _____ of Man?" _____ 9:____

Lesson 6

Standing for Truth:
A Blind Man Boasts of Jesus

What did you learn from the blind man who saw Jesus better than the Pharisees?

Read back over your answers this week. Then put an **X** in the ☐ by ideas that were new to you or that made you think differently about how a person who perseveres acts.

People who persevere in doing God's work...

☐ 1. obey Jesus' words exactly.

☐ 2. tell others what Jesus did for them personally.

☐ 3. stick to the truth, even if others say the opposite.

☐ 4. speak truth, even if it may bring consequences.

☐ 5. are determined to tell the truth over and over if needed.

☐ 6. invite others to believe in Jesus, too.

☐ 7. boldly share what they know about God.

☐ 8. discover Jesus in new ways.

☐ 9. grow in faith and worship of God.

Put an **X** in this ☐ if you can say John 9:35 from memory.

Bible Verses for Lesson 7

Selected verses from Matthew 20, 26 & 28 and Luke 18 & 24

(Jesus' came to earth to do a huge job. He had to suffer death to make a way for sinful people to be close to our perfect God. He knew exactly what God the Father wanted Him to do and began His work by telling His closest friends.)

Matthew 20:18-19

[18]"We are going up to Jerusalem, and the Son of Man will be betrayed to the chief priests and the teachers of the law. They will condemn him to death [19]and will turn him over to the Gentiles to be mocked and flogged and crucified. On the third day he will be raised to life!"

Luke 24:7

'The Son of Man must be delivered into the hands of sinful men, be crucified and on the third day be raised again.' "

Luke 18:31

[31]Jesus took the Twelve aside and told them, "We are going up to Jerusalem, and everything that is written by the prophets about the Son of Man will be fulfilled."

Matthew 26:36-46

[36]Then Jesus went with his disciples to a place called Gethsemane, and he said to them, "Sit here while I go over there and pray." [38]Then he said to them, "My soul is overwhelmed with sorrow to the point of death. Stay here and keep watch with me." [39]Going a little farther, he fell with his face to the ground and prayed, "My Father, if it is possible, may this cup be taken from me. Yet not as I will, but as you will." [40]Then he returned to his disciples and found them sleeping. "Could you men not keep watch with me for one hour?" he asked Peter. [41]"Watch and pray so that you will not fall into temptation. The spirit is willing, but the body is weak." [42]He went away a second time and prayed, "My Father, if it is not possible for this cup to be taken away unless I drink it, may your will be done." [43]When he came back, he again found them sleeping, because their eyes were heavy. [44]So he left them and went away once more and prayed the third time, saying the same thing. [45]Then he returned to the disciples and said to them, "Are you still sleeping and resting? Look, the hour is near, and the Son of Man is betrayed into the hands of sinners. [46]Rise, let us go! Here comes my betrayer!"

Matthew 26:55-56, 63-66

[55]At that time Jesus said to the crowd, "Am I leading a rebellion, that you have come out with swords and clubs to capture me? Every day I sat in the temple courts teaching, and you did not arrest me. [56]But this has all taken place that the writings of the prophets might be fulfilled." Then all the disciples deserted him and fled.

(Next Jesus was put through an unfair trial.)

[63]But Jesus remained silent. The high priest said to him, "I charge you under oath by the living God: Tell us if you are the Christ, the Son of God." [64]"Yes, it is as you say," Jesus replied. "But I say to all of you: In the future you will see the Son of Man sitting at the right hand of the Mighty One and coming on the clouds of heaven." [65]Then the high priest tore his clothes and said, "He has spoken blasphemy! Why do we need any more witnesses? Look, now you have heard the blasphemy. [66]What do you think?" "He is worthy of death," they answered.

(After more trials, they made Jesus carry a heavy wooden cross up a big hill and they crucified Him, but 3 days later He came back to life - proving He was God!)

Matthew 28:2-7

[2]There was a violent earthquake, for an angel of the LORD came down from heaven and, going to the tomb, rolled back the stone and sat on it. [3]His appearance was like lightning, and his clothes were white as snow. [4]The guards were so afraid of him that they shook and became like dead men. [5]The angel said to the women, "Do not be afraid, for I know that you are looking for Jesus, who was crucified. [6]He is not here; he has risen, just as he said. Come and see the place where he lay. [7]Then go quickly and tell his disciples: 'He has risen from the dead and is going ahead of you into Galilee. There you will see him.' Now I have told you."

Luke 24:45-53

[45]Then he opened their minds so they could understand the Scriptures. [46]He told them, "This is what is written: The Christ will suffer and rise from the dead on the third day, [47]and repentance and forgiveness of sins will be preached in his name to all nations, beginning at Jerusalem. [48]You are witnesses of these things. [49]I am going to send you what my Father has promised; but stay in the city until you have been clothed with power from on high."

[50]When he had led them out to the vicinity of Bethany, he lifted up his hands and blessed them. [51]While he was blessing them, he left them and was taken up into heaven. [52]Then they worshiped him and returned to Jerusalem with great joy. [53]And they stayed continually at the temple, praising God.

Saving the World:
Jesus Goes to the Cross for Us

Matthew 20:18-19, Luke 24:7, Luke 18:31

1. What did Jesus tell His followers He had to do? Fill in blanks in Matthew 20:18-19.

"We are going up to _____, and the Son of Man will be betrayed to the chief

priests and the teachers of the law. They will condemn him to _____ and will turn

him over to the Gentiles to be _____ and flogged (beaten) and

_____. On the _____ day he will be _____ _____ _____!"

Why Was Jesus Crucified? In Bible times Roman soldiers often killed a criminal by nailing him up on a wooden cross. So why did Jesus die like a criminal? He never sinned, never did a bad thing. He was perfect! That's the point. Jesus didn't die for His sins. He didn't have any. He died on the cross to pay for *ours* – yours and mine. (Don't worry. God won't ask anyone else to die to take away sins. Jesus did it once for all.) If Jesus had not died for us, we would not have the love and care of our perfect God. We would not be able to pray to Him for help or look forward to living in Heaven with Him. Jesus made all that possible. Thank you, Jesus!

2. What did Jesus tell His followers He had to do? Fill in blanks in Luke 24:7.

"The Son of Man must be _____ into the hands of _____ men,

be _____ and on the _____ day be _____ again."

3. Did Jesus know what He was supposed to do? (Circle one.)   YES   NO

4. Jesus was God. He knew everything, but He gave us a clue about where we need to look to find out what God wants us to do. Write Jesus' clue from Luke 18:31.

"We are going up to Jerusalem, and everything that is _____ ____ _____

_____ about the Son of Man will be fulfilled."

Making a Prophet
Only God made true prophets - people in the Bible who heard messages from God and gave them to the people. The prophet Moses gave us 5 books of the Bible. God inspired others to write the rest. Since the Bible is made of God's Words to His prophets, we can trust it today to know how God wants us to live and what He wants us to do.

Count Over & Down

So where can YOU look for direction from God? For each picture, find that picture in the letters at the right. Count the first number of letters over ➡ and the second number of letters down ⬇. Write the letter you land on in the space over the matching picture below. The first one is done for you.

❤ = 5 over & 1 down
● = 7 over & 7 down
◆ = 2 over & 1 down
▲ = 4 over & 2 down
🏠 = 3 over & 5 down
■ = 1 over & 4 down
☺ = 7 over & 1 down

```
●  N  P  ▲T  W  T  D  S
W  T  K  G  W  🏠 X  J  M
◆  D  R  T  W  P  Q  I  E
N  P  B  Y  L  ■  R  L  C
☺  W  L  D  N  E  C  W  K
I  S  ♥  K  E  P  D  E  L
L  T  K  E  S  L  I  M  B
U  E  M  Z  K  E  L  Y  D
```

<u>M</u> ___ ___ ___ ___ ___ ___

72

Mind Changers

1. A good way to find out what work God has for you is to pray and then read your Bible looking for answers. Draw lines to match each Bible verse below with the job God might ask you to do as a grown up.

teacher

Sing joyfully to the Lord, you righteous; it is fitting for the upright to praise him. (Psalm 33:1)

missionary

My heart is stirred by a noble theme as I recite my verses for the king; my tongue is the pen of a skillful writer. (Psalm 45:1)

pastor

(Speaking of using our gifts from God) If it is serving, let him serve; if it is teaching, let him teach; (Romans 12:7)

writer/speaker

Therefore go and make disciples of all nations, baptizing them in the name of the Father and of the Son and of the Holy Spirit, (Matthew 28:19)

singer

It was he who gave some to be apostles, some to be prophets, some to be evangelists, and some to be pastors and teachers, (Ephesians 4:11)

2. You must know what God wants you to do in order to persevere. Take a moment to pray and ask God what work He has planned for you. Write below what comes to mind.

___

Lesson 7 Memory Verse
Luke 24:52-53

Then they worshiped him and returned to Jerusalem with great joy.
And they stayed continually at the temple, praising God.

Lesson 7

Day 2

Saving the World:
Jesus Goes to the Cross for Us

Matthew 26:36-44

1. Circle the important thing Jesus did to prepare for His work. (Matthew 26:36).
"Sit here while I go over there and …"

                    sleep   e-mail   pray

2. Jesus was serious about praying. In 26:39 He: _____ with His face to the _____

3. Check verses 39, 42 and 44. Circle how many times Jesus prayed.   1   3   5

4. Jesus didn't just teach us to pray by example. Write the words in 41 where He commands His followers to pray.

"_____ and _____ so that you will not fall into temptation."

5. Jesus asked others to pray; should we encourage our friends to pray?   YES   NO

Mind Changers

1. Circle all the times when you pray, or write in others.

when you get up   before meals   when you have problems   at bedtime

before big tests   if you're sick if friends ask you to   before hard things

---

2. Circle one time you want to begin praying regularly and ask God to help you start.

when you get up   before meals   when you have problems   at bedtime

before big tests   if you're sick if friends ask you to   before hard things

3. Mark (or write) times when you plan to encourage others to pray by your example.

☐ praying before meals in public

☐ praying morning and evening when you're away at camp or a friend's house

☐ _____

4. Mark (or write) times when you plan to encourage others to pray with your words.

☐ offer to pray with a friend who is sad and encourage him or her to keep on praying

☐ offer to pray for a sick friend and encourage him or her to keep on praying

☐ _____

📖 Put the memory verse phrases in correct order. Write 1 by the first, 2 by the second, etc.

___ at the temple praising God.
___ and returned to Jerusalem
___ Then they worshiped him
___ with great joy.
___ And they stayed continually
(Luke 24:52-53)

Saving the World:
Jesus Goes to the Cross for Us

Matthew 26:46, 55-56, 63-65

1. After praying, Jesus was arrested. Write what His friends, the disciples, did. (56)

Then all the disciples _____ Him and _____.

2. As God, Jesus could have called angels to free Him from the guards to avoid the cross. When Jesus' friends left Him, what did He decide to do? (Circle one.)

not suffer and die on the cross for us   finish the work God the Father gave Him

3. Circle what Jesus answered when the high priest asked Him, "Tell us if you are the Christ, the Son of God." (63).

      MAYBE   NO COMMENT   YES   NO

4. Write why that upset the high priest. (65)   "He has spoken _____!"

5. Jesus knew that telling the truth about being God would get Him killed. Did that keep Him from telling the truth? (Circle one.)

            YES   NO

Blasted for Blasphemy Blasphemy means "to insult God or _falsely_ claim to be God." The high priest thought Jesus lied by claiming to be God. But Jesus told the truth! He was NOT guilty of blasphemy. Jesus was and is God. The high priest was so focused on keeping his powerful, job that He could not see the face of God standing right in front of Him.

6. After more trials, Jesus was beaten and crucified. John 19:30 tells us what happened at the end. "Jesus said, 'It is finished.'" Circle all you think Jesus meant by, "It is finished."

His suffering was done.   It was the end of time.   His sacrifice for our sins was done.

Mind Changers

1. Even though Jesus' friends ran away right before He had to do a hard thing for God, Jesus went on with His work. Circle what you would do if...

(A) You and friends are helping a neighbor pick up leaves, but they run after another friend who comes over bragging about a new game he got. Will you:

Stay and finish the work to honor God?   Run off with the others?

(B) You and friends agree to gather food for a local food bank, but on collection day it's windy and rainy. Most of the others go home. Will you:

Make an excuse and leave?   Brave the bad weather to help others?

2. Jesus told the truth, even if it brought bad consequences. Circle what you'd do.

(A) You broke a window with a baseball, but nobody saw. Will you:

Tell your mom the truth and face consequences?   Lie about not knowing who did it?

(B) You hear kids teasing a friend for going to church. You go to stand up for him. When you show up, the kids ask if you go to church, too. Will you:

Lie and say, "No" so they don't tease you?   Say, "Yes," because it's true?

3. Jesus finished His work. God gives us things to do everyday. Circle all that you are willing to promise God you will do for Him starting today.

be kind to my family   clean my room   help with chores   do homework

📖 Circle the right word in each pair
in your memory verse – Luke 24:52-53.

Then they (worshiped , left) him and returned to (Iowa , Jerusalem) with great joy. And they stayed (once , continually) at the (temple , hospital) praising God.

Saving the World:
Jesus Goes to the Cross for Us

Matthew 28:2-7, Luke 24:46-53

1. Because Jesus persevered to the cross, something amazing happened! Find all the underlined words that tell about it. (Words may be forward, backward or diagonal.)

Matthew 28:2-7

There was a violent <u>earthquake</u>, for an <u>angel</u> of the LORD came down from heaven and, going to the tomb, rolled back the stone and sat on it. His appearance was like lightning, and his clothes were white as snow. The guards were so afraid of him that they shook and became like dead men. The angel said to the women, "Do not be afraid, for I know that you are looking for <u>Jesus</u>, who was crucified. He is not here; he has <u>risen</u>, just as he said. Come and <u>see</u> the place where he lay. <u>Then go</u> quickly and <u>tell</u> his disciples: 'He has risen from the dead and is going ahead of you into Galilee. There you will see him.' Now I have told you. "

```
C C O S R E N P L P F E T L Y
F E K C M T N O I M M E O Y K
L M A N G E L I R S N O M E D
F F A R E A T H I P H U T E O
L X U I T M X D S X V I F D E
L T H G I H H S E M S U S E J
E U N P L T Q T N I S A S K W
T R T R N E O U D R S W H Y N
F M I L D S W P A E S E E T E
S N O M E D T H R K H U T E S
H U U I M M X D I X E W L U I
L M E F O G N E H T R E N P R
D C O E W G R L L R R D I R B
```

2. Mark blessings we have since Jesus persevered for us. (Matt. 28:7, Luke 24:45-53)

☐ Jesus is alive and goes ahead of you!   ☐ open minds to scriptures
☐ repentance and forgiveness of sins will be preached in His name to all nations
☐ eating all the ice cream we want   ☐ Jesus blessed His followers

3. Jesus' followers were sad when He died. Write how they felt after He rose. (52)

Then they worshiped Him and returned to Jerusalem with _____ _____.

4. Circle the things Jesus' followers get to enjoy because Jesus persevered. (52-53)

worshiping Him   great joy   easy life   praising God

Mind Changers

1. Our doing good works for God can't earn a place in heaven, but Jesus' work brought wonderful blessings for Him and us. What blessings could you or others enjoy if you do the work God gives you? Draw lines to match each WORK to its BLESSING.

WORK   BLESSING

Set the table cheerfully   Be able to find things easily in your room

Pray with a friend to accept Jesus Enjoy a cozy family meal

Keep your room clean   Joy knowing your friend will be in heaven
                                    with Jesus someday – forever

2. What work do you feel God is telling you to start doing today? _____

3. Write of a time you enjoyed praising God. (If you can't think of one, ask Him to help you <u>want</u> to praise Him.) _____

📖 **Write in what's missing to finish your memory verse.**

Then they _____ him and returned to Jerusalem with great _____ . And they _____ continually at the temple _____ God. (_____ 24:52-53)

79

Saving the World:
Jesus Goes to the Cross for Us

What did you learn from Jesus persevering to the cross for us?

Read back over your answers this week. Then put an **X** in the □ by ideas that were new to you or that made you think differently about how a person who perseveres acts.

People who persevere like Jesus in doing the work God has for them...

□ 1. have a clear picture of the work God's given them.

□ 2. go to God's Word to learn God's will.

□ 3. pray hard and often.

□ 4. encourage others to pray.

□ 5. stick to God's plan, even if friends run away.

□ 6. speak the truth, even if people don't believe it.

□ 7. do everything they can to finish God's work.

□ 8. enjoy more blessings than one can ask or imagine.

□ 9. worship God with great joy and praise Him continually.

Put an **X** in this □ if you can say Luke 24:52-53 from memory.

Bible Verses for Lesson 8

Selected verses from Acts 13, 14, 21 & 28

(Paul killed Christians until he heard Jesus personally and got a job from Him!)

Acts 13:47-52 (Paul speaking)

[47]For this is what the LORD has commanded us:" 'I have made you a light for the Gentiles, that you may bring salvation to the ends of the earth.'" [48]When the Gentiles heard this, they were glad and honored the word of the LORD; and all who were appointed for eternal life believed. [49]The word of the LORD spread through the whole region.
(But some Jews drove Paul and Barnabas away.)

[51]So they shook the dust from their feet in protest against them and went to Iconium.
[52]And the disciples were filled with joy and with the Holy Spirit.

Acts 14:1, 4-11, 14-15

[1]At Iconium Paul and Barnabas went as usual into the Jewish synagogue. There they spoke so effectively that a great number of Jews and Gentiles believed. [4]The people of the city were divided; some sided with the Jews, others with the apostles. [5]There was a plot afoot among the Gentiles and Jews, together with their leaders, to mistreat them and stone them. [6]But they found out about it and fled to the Lycaonian cities of Lystra and Derbe and to the surrounding country, [7]where they continued to preach the good news.

[8]In Lystra there sat a man crippled in his feet, who was lame from birth and had never walked. [9]He listened to Paul as he was speaking. Paul looked directly at him, saw that he had faith to be healed [10]and called out, "Stand up on your feet!" At that, the man jumped up and began to walk. [11]When the crowd saw what Paul had done, they shouted in the Lycaonian language, "The gods have come down to us in human form!"

[14]But when the apostles Barnabas and Paul heard of this, they tore their clothes and rushed out into the crowd, shouting: [15]"Men, why are you doing this? We too are only men, human like you. We are bringing you good news, telling you to turn from these worthless things to the living God, who made heaven and earth and sea and everything in them.

Acts 21:27, 31, 33, 37, 40

[27]When the seven days were nearly over, some Jews from the province of Asia saw Paul at the temple. They stirred up the whole crowd and seized him, [31]While they were trying to kill him, news reached the commander of the Roman troops that the whole city of Jerusalem was in an uproar. [33]The commander came up and arrested him and ordered him to be bound with two chains. Then he asked who he was and what he had done.

[37]As the soldiers were about to take Paul into the barracks, he asked the commander, "May I say something to you?" [40]Having received the commander's permission, Paul stood on the steps and motioned to the crowd. When they were all silent, he said to them in Aramaic:

(Paul told how Jesus' Words changed his life and could change theirs.)

Acts 28:14-16, 30-31

[14]There we found some brothers who invited us to spend a week with them. And so we came to Rome. [15]The brothers there had heard that we were coming, and they traveled as far as the Forum of Appius and the Three Taverns to meet us. At the sight of these men Paul thanked God and was encouraged. [16]When we got to Rome, Paul was allowed to live by himself, with a soldier to guard him. [30]For two whole years Paul stayed there in his own rented house and welcomed all who came to see him. [31]Boldly and without hindrance he preached the kingdom of God and taught about the LORD Jesus Christ.

Lesson 8   Day 1

Persuading the World:
Paul Tells Gentiles Jesus is Alive

Acts 13:47-52

1. Write the name of the people for whom Jesus made Paul a "light." (Acts. 13:47)

"I have made you a light for the _____, that you may bring salvation to the ends of the earth."

2. Circle the same word in this answer Paul heard from Jesus when Paul prayed.
"Go; I will send you far away to the Gentiles."

Salvation for Gentiles? A "Gentile" is anyone who is not Jewish, not from Israel. For years God told His chosen people, Israel, that they had to be saved from their sins in order to be close to Him. In fact, all Israel was waiting for Messiah to come – the One who would save or deliver them from their sins. When Jesus died on the cross and came back to life He gave "salvation" to all who believe in Him. To Gentiles, these were all new ideas so Jesus told Paul to go far away and teach them.

3. Circle two things Paul knew for sure about the work God gave him (47). Paul would:

stay where he was   go far away   talk to Americans

have an easy life   get rich   talk to Gentiles about salvation

4. Do you think Paul had a clear idea of what Jesus wanted Him to do?   YES   NO

5. Circle what happened when Paul began the work Jesus gave him. (Acts 13:47-49)

Gentiles were glad.   Gentiles cried.   Gentiles honored God's Word

Some believed.   Gentiles had a party.   The Word of the Lord spread.

6. Did ALL people react the same way to Paul's message? Circle T (true) or F (false).

T F All Jews believed in Jesus.   T F Some Jews drove Paul and Barnabas away.

7. When doing God's work, what were the disciples filled with? (Circle two.) (52)

   pop corn   joy   jelly beans   fear   Holy Spirit

Mind Changers

1. Take a moment to pray. Ask God if there is anything He wants you to do today. Listen quietly and write what comes to mind here. _____

2. Who will you tell about what God is teaching you in this study or doing in your life?

_____   _____   _____

Lesson 8 Memory Verse
Acts 13:47

For this is what the Lord has commanded us: "'I have made you a light for

the Gentiles, that you may bring salvation to the ends of the earth.'"

Lesson 8

Persuading the World:
Paul Tells Gentiles Jesus is Alive

Acts 13:51, 14:1-15, 28:16

1. Circle all the places Paul went to teach about Jesus. (13:51, 14:6, 28:16)

Florida	Iconium	the moon	Nebraska	Lystra
Canada	Derbe	grocery store	Rome	China

2. Did Paul complain about where God sent Him? YES NO

3. Who did the people say Paul was when the crippled man walked? (14:11)

When the crowd saw what Paul had done, they shouted in the Lyconian language, "The
_____ have down to us in human form!"

4. Circle the things Paul and Barnabas did in verses 14-15.

said, Thank you."   tore their clothes   accepted their gifts

rushed into the crowd   shouted, "We are only men! Turn from these worthless
                           things to the living God!

Does God Heal Everyone? God never changes. He can still heal anyone, but He doesn't always choose to. Sometimes He allows sickness or hard things to get our attention or to help us depend on Him. God knows that our character and being close to Him are more important than our comfort. The Bible says, "As the heavens are higher than the earth, so are my ways higher than your ways and my thoughts than your thoughts." (Isaiah 55:9) We may not always understand God, but we can always trust Him.

5. Circle who Paul wanted the people to praise for the man's healing.   Paul   God

Mind Changers

1. Circle 3 places that you might find it hard to go to serve God when you grow up.

hospital   Africa   war zone   poor neighborhood

homeless shelter   China   retirement home for older people

2. Write a prayer asking God to give you a willing heart to go wherever He sends you.

_____

3. Circle or write in things you could tell others that God did for you.

healed you from a sickness   caused you to believe in Jesus as your Savior

spoke to you in the Bible   answered a prayer in a special way

helped you tell a friend about Him   helped you persevere in doing this workbook

_____

Circle the right word in each pair
in your memory verse – Acts 13:47.

For this is what the (boss , Lord) has commanded us:
"'I have made you a light for the (Gentiles , frogs)
that you may bring (umbrellas , salvation) to the ends of the earth.'"

Lesson 8

Day 3

Persuading the World:
Paul Tells Gentiles Jesus is Alive

Acts 21:27-40

1. When God sent Paul to Jerusalem to teach about Jesus, what happened? (21:27-33)

Some Jews "_____ ____ the whole crowd and _____ him,"

While they were trying to _____ him,

The commander came up and _____ him and ordered him to be _____

2. After that trouble, did Paul keep quiet or keep speaking truth? (Circle one.) (37)

Paul said, "May I say something to you?"   Paul said, "I take back all I said."

3. Because he was arrested, Paul got to speak of Jesus to a governor, a king and many other powerful leaders. He even got to the center of the Roman empire where top ruler, Caesar, reigned. One phrase appears in both verses below showing that Paul asked to go to Rome on purpose because that's what God wanted. Draw lines under that phrase.

"You have appealed to Caesar. To Caesar you will go!" (Acts 25:12)
"This man could have been set free if he had not appealed to Caesar." (Acts 26:32)

4. Did Paul cooperate with God in going where God wanted him?   YES   NO

Mind Changers

1. You must know truth before you can tell others. The Bible is the best source of truth. Draw lines to match false things people say with true Bible verses.

Jesus was just a good man.   All have sinned and fall short of the glory of God.

Most people are good.   No one comes to the Father except through (Jesus).

There are many ways to heaven.   Jesus is the Christ, the Son of God.

Do the Math!

Solve the math problems. Then use the key below to fill in matching letters.

$$\overline{\quad\quad}\quad \overline{\quad\quad}\quad \overline{\quad\quad}\quad \overline{\quad\quad}\quad \overline{\quad\quad}\quad \overline{\quad\quad}\quad \overline{\quad\quad}\quad \overline{\quad\quad}$$

$1 + 3 \quad\quad 2 + 4 \quad\quad 6 - 3 \quad\quad 4 - 4 \quad\quad 3 + 2 \quad\quad 1 + 1 \quad\quad 0 + 1 \quad\quad 4 - 2$

KEY   If your answer is: Then write the letter:

0	W
1	R
2	E
3	Y
4	A
5	H
6	N

NOW - Write the word you got for an answer in the blank below and then answer the question.

Are you willing to go _____ to serve God?   (Circle.)   YES   NO

Cross out wrong words in your memory verse.
Write correct words above.

For this is what the Lord has told us: "'I have made you a target for the

Gentiles, that you may bring pizza to the ends of the line.'" (Acts 13:47)

Lesson 8

Day 4

Persuading the World:
Paul Tells Gentiles Jesus is Alive

Acts 28:15-16, 30-31

1. Paul persevered though hard times by staying focused on God's plan. Find all the things Paul suffered in the word search. (Words may be forward, backward or diagonal.) Read 2 Corinthians 11:22-33 in your Bible to hear Paul's whole speech!

prison	flogged	lashes	beaten	stoned
danger	hunger	cold	arrested	shipwrecked

```
D C O S T V N K C R F E T L Y F S
L D I M M E O Y K K C E T N O H T
O D E G G O L F W S N O M E I D O
C F I D E A A H R P H U T P O E N
X D I X V I S D E H U U W M M T E
P T H G I E H S S M M R L W J S D
N L S Z L T E T D I E A S K W E Y
E R T R N E S O N C S W H Y P R T
T E R E S E N T K I L D S W P R V
A L U Q L M E E I E T E F L R A N
E C O E W G D L L R R D I R I K T
B I H U N G E R C U F P A A S X T
P N C O T E W B W M D U L U O K I
A T N D E P T H F I H U A F N R C
F F I D N R S W D A N G E R K W P
S R E N I E H S T H G I E H S M I
M E V I E T E F L K T H R P H U T
```

2. Because Paul persevered for God, write blessings Paul enjoyed at Rome. (28:15-16)

The _____ there had heard that we were coming and traveled as far as the

Forum of Appius and the Three Taverns to _____ us. At the _____ of these men

Paul thanked God and was _____. When we got to Rome, Paul was allowed

to live _____ _____, with a soldier to guard him.

3. Circle T (true) or F (false) to describe how God worked out the details of Paul telling
Gentiles in Rome about Jesus. (30-31)

T F   Paul preached for 2 days   T F   Paul preached 2 whole years
T F   Paul was in prison   T F   Paul was in his own rented house
T F   Paul welcomed all   T F   Paul couldn't have visitors
T F   Paul had to keep quiet   T F   Paul preached boldly
T F   Paul preached about Jesus   T F   Paul preached of God's kingdom

4. How could Paul, an arrested criminal, have so much freedom and influence?! Mark
all that you think are right.

___ Teaching Gentiles about Jesus was God's plan and God's plan can't be stopped.
___ Paul was lucky.
___ God showed His power in Paul's life because Paul persevered in doing God's work.

Mind Changers

1. Draw lines to ways you could see God's power in your life as you persevere in the work He gives you?

IF YOU…   GOD…

Ask Jesus to be your Savior   may allow you to know your friend will go to heaven

Study your Bible daily   may show you amazing answers to your prayers

Tell a friend about Jesus   will show Himself to you in His Word in new ways

Pray to Jesus everyday   will begin to make you more like Jesus

2. Take a minute to ask Jesus what He wants you to do after studying this lesson. Then listen for His answer and write it below.

_____

 Write in what's missing to finish your memory verse.

For this is what the _____ has commanded us: "'I have _____ you a

_____ for the _____, that you may _____ salvation

to the ends of the _____.'" (_____ ___: 47)

Persuading the World:
Paul Tells Gentiles Jesus is Alive

What did you learn from Paul being faithful to carry God's message far away?

Read back over your answers this week. Then put an **X** in the □ by ideas that were new to you or that made you think differently about how a person who perseveres acts.

People who persevere in doing God's work...

□ 1. have a clear picture of the work God's given them.

□ 2. tell others what God is doing.

□ 3. are willing to serve God wherever He sends them.

□ 4. don't take praise for themselves that belongs to God.

□ 5. speak the truth, even if it makes them unpopular.

□ 6. cooperate with God in going wherever He wants.

□ 7. endure hardship by staying focused on God's plan.

□ 8. enjoy God's blessings as they do His work.

□ 9. see God's power as He works out His plan through them.

Put an **X** in this □ if you can say Acts 13:47 from memory.

If You Want Jesus to Be Your Savior...

Believe This –

• God is perfect and holy.

"As for God, his way is perfect; the word of the LORD is flawless. He is a shield for all who take refuge in him." (2 Samuel 22:31)

• Every person who ever lived has done bad things. (We call those sins.) So no one deserves to be close to God or to go to heaven.

"for all have sinned and fall short of the glory of God." (Romans 3:23)

• We cannot do enough good things to earn our way to God.

"All of us have become like one who is unclean, and all our righteous acts are like filthy rags; we all shrivel up like a leaf, and like the wind our sins sweep us away." (Isaiah 64:6)

• But God loved us so much that He paid the penalty for our sins with His perfect justice and love. Jesus died on the cross in our place – so we would not have punishment, but forgiveness.

"For God so loved the world that He gave His one and only Son that whoever believes in Him shall not perish, but have eternal life." (John 3:16)

• Then Jesus rose from the dead to prove that He is God and to give us the promise that we will live forever with Him in a perfect place called Heaven if we accept Him as Savior on earth.

"For what I received I passed on to you as of first importance: that Christ died for our sins according to the Scriptures, that he was buried, that he was raised on the third day according to the Scriptures, and that he appeared to Peter, and then to the Twelve." (1 Corinthians 15:3-5)

• Your sins are forgiven and you have a place as a child of God when you **thank** Jesus for dying for *your* sins, **believe** He came back to life and **choose** to follow His ways with His help.

for "Everyone who calls on the name of the LORD will be saved." (Rom. 10:13)

And then...

If You Want Jesus to Be Your Savior...

Pray This –

Dear God,
I am sorry for my sins. Thank you, Jesus, for dying on the cross to take my punishment and for rising from the dead. Thank you for forgiving my sins. I invite you, Jesus, to lead me in a new way of life. With your help, I will persevere in serving You.

Tell a Parent –

If you prayed that prayer, this is an exciting day! Share the big news with a parent and write down the date in the special place below. You are now part of the family of God who will live with Him forever. You may not feel different, but God's Word says that He has begun to change you into someone new. We can always trust God's Word.

"Therefore, if anyone is in Christ, he is a new creation; the old has gone, the new has come!" (2 Corinthians 5:17)

"being confident of this, that He who began a good work in you will carry it on to completion until the day of Christ Jesus." (Philippians 1:6)

Welcome to the Family! If you prayed to accept Jesus as your Savior...congratulations!

I prayed to ask Jesus to be my Savior on

_____ _____ , _____!
     (month)   (date)   (year)

Visit www.life-changingwords.com
**for tools to help you live a changed life, as well as other Bible studies and resources.
Look for stories from others whose lives have been changed, too.**